Do Your Part: How You Can Fight Global Warming

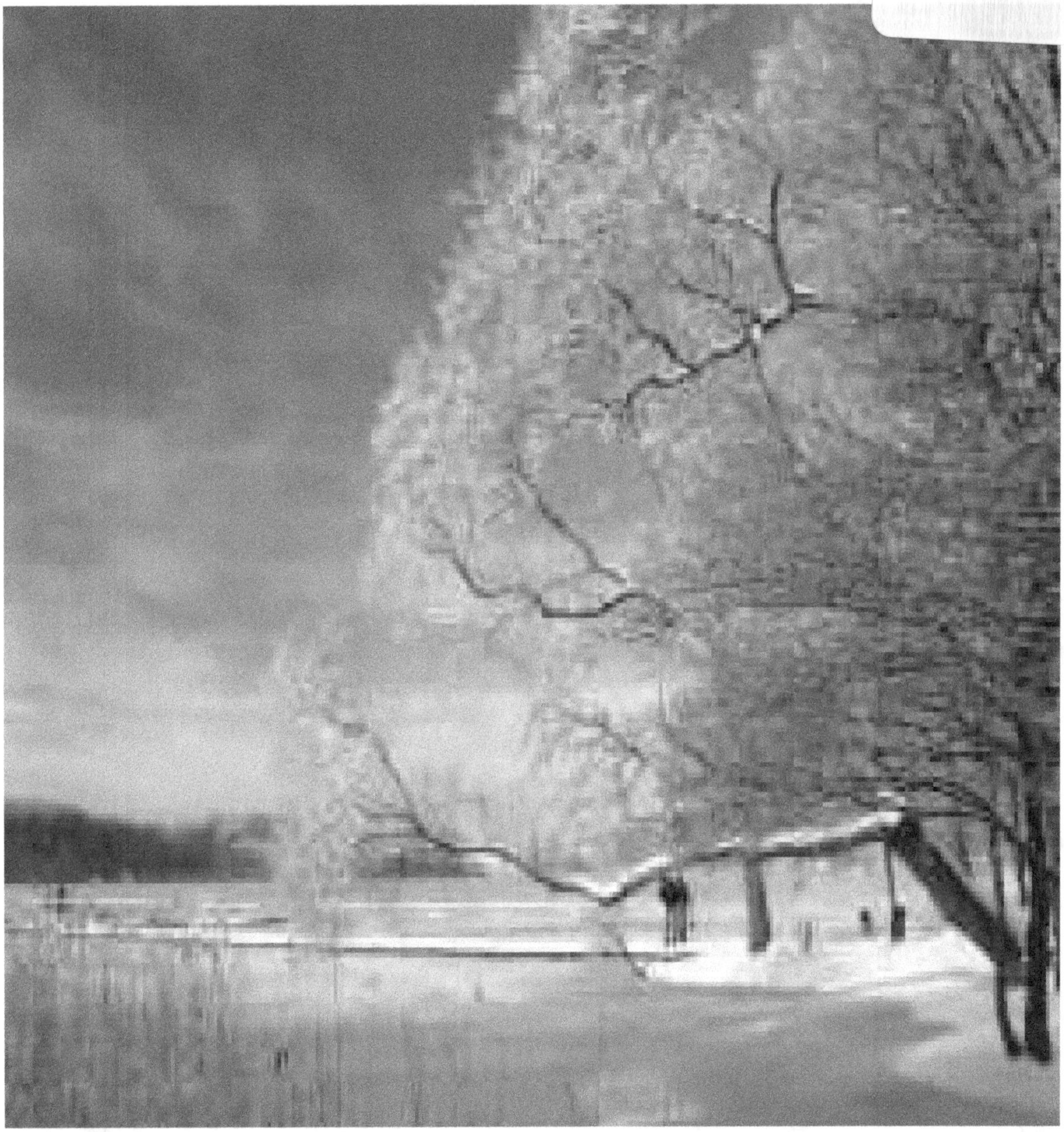

ISBN Number: 1434810305

Published by CreateSpace

Table of Contents

Introduction

Over the last year or so, many people have begun to focus their attention on the very real problem of Global Warming. While environmentalists and others have known about global warming for quite some time, it has taken the issue awhile to capture the public's attention. For many years, there were doubts that the problem even existed. But recently, all but a few scientists agree that the problem is very real and that the earth faces severe problems if we don't act immediately to begin to reverse the damage of global warming.

One of the things that have raised public awareness of this issue is the movie, *An Inconvenient Truth*, produced and presented by former vice-president Al Gore. The former senator from Tennessee got interested in the problem when he was in college, over forty years ago, and he has maintained his interest in the face of many nay-sayers and critiques throughout the years. But with the release of *An Inconvenient Truth*, he is getting global warming the attention it deserves. Other events have also served to raise the public's awareness that global warming might be a problem—the terrible hurricanes that have battered the Gulf Coast of the United States and other international locations, as well as other unusual weather. Many regions have experienced extreme heat or cold or strong storms. Hearing about natural disasters brings home immediately the idea that perhaps something is amiss on our beautiful green and blue planet.

Global warming is a big problem. Many people feel that there is no more important issue to work on—after all, if our planet is our only home. Without a clean, healthy earth on which to live, we have nothing. Yet to the average citizen, it may seem like such an overwhelming issue that there's really nothing anyone can do. However, nothing could be further from the truth. The good news is that there is plenty all of us can do. The even better news is that there are many effective activities that aren't particularly difficult to accomplish. Best of all, many of these activities which positively impact global warming will improve your quality of life.

This report will give you many, many ideas about simple steps you can take to help the problem of global warming. We'll talk about energy conservation (it's not nearly as daunting as it seems), being a green commuter, recycling (many communities are making this a breeze for consumers), water conservation, shopping green, and even simple things like the benefits of planting a garden. You will find activities that you can involve the entire family in, things to do that you'll enjoy. You'll feel better about the lifestyle choices you are making because you will be certain that you are leaving a lighter footprint on this earth. And that is what it is all about.

Before we get into the information about the activities and ideas for fighting global warming, first we are going to explain it (don't worry, its all in layman's terms). We will discuss what global warming actually is, how it affects you and your family, and what is being done before we get into the lengthy section on what you can do.

A couple more notes before we get started: at the end of each section you will find a handy bullet-point reference list that recaps the ideas. We want to make it as easy as possible for you to follow through on the ideas listed here. Also, at the end of this special report you will find a page of resources, including websites and organizations where you can go to find out more information.

Okay. Are you ready to get going? Let's jump right in—the earth is in peril and there's no time to waste.

What Is Global Warming?

The simplest definition of global warming is that it is an increase in the surface temperature of the earth. The term that we are all getting used to hearing now most often means artificial warming of the earth that is due to *greenhouse gases*. What are greenhouse gases? These are emissions from human activities such as driving cars and using electrical appliances. The biggest culprit is *carbon dioxide*, which gets trapped in the atmosphere and makes everything warmer, like a heavy blanket. You may have heard this called the *greenhouse effect*.

There is more carbon dioxide currently trapped in the atmosphere than there has been in the last 650,000 years. You read that right—650,000 years. Consider that most of that carbon dioxide is there because of our human activities and you start to get the picture. A little bit of greenhouse gas in the atmosphere is not all bad. After all, we do need some warmth! The natural ecosystem which traps the correct amount of warmth in the atmosphere is what gives us fresh air, clean water, and the natural weather systems.

However, we've overloaded it so much with the emissions from our cars, and power plants, and over-consumptive lifestyles that it is endangering our planet. The earth's surface temperature has risen by about one degree Fahrenheit over the last century, and that is expected to accelerate. In general, the earth's ecosystem is changing, thanks largely to the humans who inhabit it.

Another phrase you'll hear a lot is *climate change*. It's important to bear in mind that climate changes occur naturally over the centuries and millennia, however, the current warming that we are experiencing is way more extreme than could be accounted for in normal fluctuation. Changes that scientists had forecast to occur as the result of global warming have already begun.

And many scientists believe that severe climate changes and some of the catastrophic weather that often accompanies it are the result of our increased global warming. There has been a marked increase in the number of category four and five hurricanes over the last few years. That's because hurricanes are formed over warm sea water, and as the water temperatures of the oceans rise, more killer storms are created. Many other changes occur from warmer sea temperatures, such as the melting of the polar icecaps.

One of the results of the melting polar ice caps is that the oceans are beginning to rise. When you consider that most of the world's population lives on or near coasts, you can start to see the problem. If we continue at our current rate of spewing greenhouse gases into the air, the oceans are expected to rise six feet in 100 years—or less. Rising sea levels threaten massive physical devastation and damage to economies worldwide. And consider this—while the United States has only four percent of the world's population, it is responsible for 22% of the greenhouse gas emissions.

One of the first things that occur as temperatures rise is that more disease-carrying insects and rodents thrive. While we normally associate diseases such as malaria and encephalitis with other continents, we'll be seeing a lot more of them in the future, right here in the United States, if global warming continues at its current rate. This has already started to happen, and doctors at the Harvard Medical Center have linked outbreaks of various diseases such as the Hantavirus directly to climate change.

How Does Global Warming Affect Me?

Perhaps you are reading all this and wondering what the big deal is. After all, these are big concepts. If you don't live in a part of the country impacted by hurricanes, maybe you feel you don't have much to worry about. Or perhaps you live in a very cold part of the country and you would welcome global warming. But nothing could be further than the truth—global warming affects us all.

We only have one planet and one place for us all to live. So far, scientists have not found any other planets that are habitable without massive intervention that is beyond our economic means. So, we are stuck here on earth and we need to make sure that we are actively preserving this beautiful planet.

Climate change means more than warmer winters. (And, for the record, many of those bitterly cold winters and huge storms parts of the country have been getting are the direct result of global warming.) Climate change means that certain regions will no longer be able to sustain farmlands or grow the same crops. It  means changing precipitation and regional climates that can affect human and animal health and welfare. Some changes that might happen would include expanding desserts, drier soils, more intense rainstorms and faster evaporation of the water from them. None of these results are good for the health for the planet or its inhabitants.

The above-mentioned diseases will be harder and harder to contain and control, and some of them can be very deadly. In the United States, we don't have to worry too much about insect-born diseases. We are used to the luxury of spending time outdoors without fretting. But that may soon change as more and more of the populace becomes prone to unusual illnesses.

Here's another startling statistic: 800,000 people a year die from sicknesses caused by air pollution, half of those in China, which is second after the United States in carbon dioxide emissions, according to the World Health Organization.

 Other changes from global warming that will have an extreme adverse impact on us include more frequent and intense heat waves and prolonged drought, and more wildfires. Some predict that the Artic Ocean will be ice free by 2050, and more than a million species worldwide will be driven to extinction by that same year. Already many animals have begun changing their habits and habitats, moving closer to the poles.

While we are already seeing the results of climate change and global warming in our own lives, it is our children and grand children who will be living in a vastly altered landscape. Do we want to be known as the people who stood idly by and did nothing to improve the lives of future generations? The Native Americans have long had a philosophy that everything they do should be considered in light of the impact it will have on all the generations to come. Tread lightly on the planet is a philosophy that we can all follow.

What is being done?

Programs to stem the tide of global warming are being implemented on the federal, state and local levels. The United States Environmental Protection Agency (EPA) is the lead federal agency involved in this program and it is partnering with state, local and private agencies to address the challenges of global warming while strengthening the economy. Also at the federal level, the U.S. Global Change Research Program is researching global warming, its effects and what we can do to stop it.

Many state agencies are creating programs to reduce greenhouse emissions, and local governments are creating curbside recycling programs and encouraging businesses to go green with a variety of incentives.

How about on the global level? While the U.S. is responsible for a huge preponderance of the greenhouse emissions, it's certainly not our problem alone. The U.S. government is working with other countries through the United Nations. The program is called the United Nations Framework Convention on Climate Change. The Kyoto Protocol is an international and binding agreement that many are entering into as a way to reduce greenhouse gases worldwide. While the U.S. under the current administration has refused to sign this legally binding agreement, many local cities have done so and you can contact the mayor of your city to find out what's been done where you live.

One of the activities of the Kyoto Protocol program is to support countries and regions in coping with the current effects of the crisis. While there is much we can do to prevent future effects of global warming, we must also be aware that damage has already been done. Because of this, we must minimize the current impacts. Some of the ways this is being done is through prevention. For instance, building flood walls and moving populations out of low-lying floodplains is one recommendation. They also recommend "focusing on vulnerability," that is, identifying populations and areas that will be most at risk from climate change and global warming. Of course, more research is an ongoing necessity, as is flexibility and funding for this research. The forecasts of what will be needed on the broadest levels are fascinating—it's essential that we start actually thinking differently to solve this problem.

It is true that some governmental bodies and agencies, as well as private concerns, have been slow to realize that there is a problem and even slower to act upon it. One of the key concerns is financial. Going green on every level does cost more upfront. However, study after study has shown that these higher upfront costs actually result in huge savings down the road, because green policies have such a positive impact on health and lifestyle. For instance, a recent climate change conference held in Bangkok affirmed that burning cleaner fuels resulted in health benefits that saved money. The World Health Organization recommends that governments should consider the increased savings in health costs if they aren't dealing with the direct results of global warming—heat waves, disease, and water scarcity. More and more, governments around the world are recognizing that going green will result in long-term savings.

Finally, many organizations are working hard to reduce the impact of this problem. One of the most prominent is called Global Green, which is the U.S. arm of Green Cross International, a group started by former Russian president Mikhail Gorbachev in 1993. He was inspired to act by the 1992 Green Summit in Rio de Janeiro. The group's mission "is to create a sustainable future by cultivating harmonious relationships between humans and the environment." It focuses on stemming global climate change by encouraging green building, eliminating weapons of mass destruction, and providing clean drinking water for the 2.4 billion people who lack it. President Gorbachev's vision is to create a new approach to the environmental crisis by connecting humans back to their environment.

There are many other organizations, both public and private, who are working very hard on this problem. They include the Environmental Defense, Stop Global Warming Now, and others. Please note that we have compiled an extensive list of organizations and resources on global warming at the end of this report. You'll find links to websites of all these groups and many other agencies there.

What Can I Do To Help Stop Global Warming?

Are you ready for some startling statistics? In the United States, 6.6 tons of greenhouse gases are emitted *per person* every year. We're not getting any better at this, as this figure rose 3.4% from 1990 to 1997. Most of these emissions come from the burning of fossil fuels to power our cars and light our homes and buildings. According to the EPA, this accounts for 82% of the emissions, a hefty chunk. The rest comes from raising livestock, natural gas pipelines, coal, industrial chemicals, and methane from waste in landfills. With figures like these, it's probably not much of a surprise that currently the U.S. emits more greenhouse gases per person than any other country on earth—though the rates do vary widely by state and region.

From these statistics you can easily see that there are three main areas where you can make a huge impact on global warming. These three areas are how much electricity we use, the waste we process, and the transportation choices we make. As consumers, we can cut down up to 32% of the emissions we spew into the air, just by making smart choices. The rest comes from industry and other sources, and we can have an impact on that by lobbying governments to come up with stricter standards.

One of the words you'll hear a lot when looking into global warming is *sustainability*. Its one of the new buzz words and it's a good one. Wikipedia defines the word as "an attempt to provide the best outcomes for the human and natural environments both now and into the future." The EPA defines it as "the ability to achieve continuing economic prosperity while protecting the natural systems of the planet and providing a high quality of life for its people." These definitions both embrace taking stewardship of the planet, its people, and the best quality of life for all—which is what taking action to ease global warming is all about.

The experts agree: the overall recommendation is for rapid transition to energy efficiency and renewable energy sources. But what does this mean? And how can the average consumer add such practices to their everyday life? That's where this report comes in.

We have compiled a list of actions, both large and small that you can take to help prevent global warming. If you are feeling overwhelmed, don't be. You can start small, taking one little step, and then expand your awareness and commitment to the cause. Bit by bit you'll be replacing old habits and before you know you'll be proud to call yourself a green citizen. You may even feel compelled to become an activist on the part of the planet. Our list of resources can help you with that, too.

Are you ready? We've got a lot of ground to cover, so let's get going. Don't forget the handy checklists at the end of each section, which gives you a quick reference of things to do immediately. You can refer to these lists if you want to get going right away, and then go back later and read the background information. The most important thing is to take action as soon as possible.

Energy conservation

We're going to discuss two kinds of conservation—both energy and water. But let's get started with energy conservation, which can range from the simple act of changing your light bulbs to more comprehensive activities like purchasing green power.

United States households alone are responsible for 21% of the global warming pollution that occurs in the world. This is more than the entire global warming output of the United Kingdom. It is clear we are not doing a very good job at energy conservation. Yet energy-conscious families can reduce their emissions by two-thirds with some simple choices.

Turn Off Lights and Appliances

The easiest way to start conserving energy is to turn off lights, appliances, computers, televisions, and gadgets, when not in use. We are spoiled. We have such abundance that we can waste it. Most of us have gotten out of the simple habit of switching off a light when we leave the room. Our grandmothers and grandfathers always turned off the lights and would be horrified if we didn't.
They did it for reasons of money but there was wisdom in their penny-pinching ways. We are blessed to have, for the most part; plentiful and cheap sources of energy which has led us to take it for granted and over-use it.

If you think that this simple act is not going to make much difference, consider this: the energy output of the average American home generated by fossil fuels puts more carbon dioxide into the air than two cars. Other things you can do include not running your washing machine and dishwasher at peak energy demand times of 5:00 AM to 9:00 AM and 4:00 to 7:00 PM. When first purchasing these appliances, buy Energy Star approved brands. (You'll find much more information on green shopping below.) And how about the simple option of pulling your shades and blinds shut at night? This can help prevent energy leaks.

Something you might not have considered is the energy drains you have in your house from unexpected sources. For instance, toasters and cell phone chargers are toting up kilowatt hours the entire time they are plugged in. One simple way to deal with this problem is to use power strips where possible, for instance, in the family room. You can plug in the television and DVD player and video games to the power strip, and then simply turn the power strip off when none of those items are in use. Unplugging un-used electronics can prevent 1,000 pounds of carbon dioxide from contributing to global warming, and save you up to $256 per year.

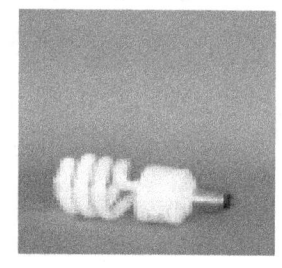

Adjust Your Thermostat

Next, consider adjusting your thermostat. Set your thermostat to 68 degrees during the day and turn it down to 55 degrees at night. For each degree you turn down your thermostat, you save up to 5% of your heating costs. Grandma would be proud—and the earth will thank you, too.

Replace Light Bulbs

One excellent way to create huge savings in energy and money is to replace your current light bulbs with Compact Florescent Bulbs or CFBs. A CFB is four times more energy efficient than an incandescent bulb, and it will provide the same lighting. If you choose to replace 3 of your frequently used light bulbs with CFBs, you can prevent 300 pounds of carbon dioxide from going into the air—and save $60 a year. That is a huge savings for such a small action. CFBs cost a bit more upfront, but they are extremely long lasting. All you have to do to realize how inefficient traditional light bulbs are is touch one. It's hot, right? Therein lays the problem—they put out more heat than light. This is where CFBs come in.

If your idea of a florescent light bulb is the old tubes that buzzed, never fear. The new CFBs are a much different thing completely. They now produce the same kind of warm light you love from incandescents, and they use much less electricity. This, in turn, means lower electric bills and less global warming pollution. It will also lower your cooling bills in the summer, because they burn so much cooler. If you tried CFBs in the past and were dissatisfied with them, please try again—they are much improved. While it may seem like a minor contribution to change to CFBs, consider this: if every household changed just three bulbs, it would equal taking 3.5 million cars off the road!

Here are some tips to get you going on changing out your light bulbs to CFBs. Start by committing to replace all incandescent bulbs with CFBs as they burn out. Use them in all your portable table and floor lamps. At first, you will need to carefully consider the sizes and shapes available, but soon you'll be familiar with what's available and it will be easier. As more and more consumers learn about CFBs and begin to purchase them, the selection is growing at home improvement and electrical supply stores. For wattage, a good guideline is to choose a CFB that is one-quarter the watts of a traditional bulb. That would mean, for instance, that if you usually use a 60-watt bulb, you would require a 15-watt CFB. They are also available in dimmers and some work in three-way lamps. Your best bet is to spend some time browsing at the store to see what's available. One more

 thing to be aware of: the most energy-efficient bulbs carry the label of Energy Star, which is the government-backed rating program.

If you have spot lighting in your home, you might want to consider using a CFB with a reflector. This will provide you with a much directed light while saving energy. You will also want to replace any torchiere fixtures that generally take halogen light bulbs with compact florescent torchieres, which  can result in a savings of up to 60% to 80%. Another simple thing to consider doing is letting more daylight in—just as it is good to shut your drapes and blinds at night, to hold energy in, during the day you want to keep them open to provide natural light. If you are a fiend for privacy, you can decorate your windows with loose-weave drapes that will allow light in, while keeping prying eyes out.

And, don't stop with just your indoor lighting. Use outdoor lighting with a photocell unit or put it on a timer so that they will automatically be turned off during the day. Just say no to decorative outdoor gas lamps. The energy burned by eight of these babies, burning year round, takes the same amount of energy as it does to heat an entire home with natural gas for a whole winter! Also bear in mind that CFBs are great to use outside because they are so long lasting.

You might also want to take the CFB pledge at www.environmentaldefense.org. You can go to a special page that allows you to make a personal action pledge to swap out your bulbs. They are working on getting one million pledges, and as of this writing were close to 224,000 bulbs being swapped out (which equals nearly 242 million pounds of carbon dioxide being spewed into the air). When your CFB burns out you will want to recycle it rather than throw it out. This is because the CFBs contain small amounts of mercury. This sound like a bad thing—after all, we all know mercury is poison. But there's actually much less in a CFB than there is a thermometer, for instance, and burning a CFB actually prevents releasing more mercury into the air by coal burning plants.

Purchase Green Power

Look into purchasing green power. Many local utility companies are providing this as an option for its customers. Currently, more than 50% or power companies in the United  States offer green power as an option. If you live in an area where retail electricity is allowed, you can buy your green power from an alternative source. If you buy energy through a regulated utility, many of these companies offer green energy and have graduated rate schemes to accommodate it. You'll pay a premium for purchasing all green power. Then there is generally a middle of the road option which is a little cheaper and is a combination of green power and traditional power. Or you can stick with your basic bill. But now that you are aware of the perils of global warming, aren't you willing to pay just a few pennies more a day to help prevent it?

What are green power programs? It refers to energy-efficient power sources that emit little or no carbon dioxide into the air, and therefore doesn't contribute to the problem of global warming. Some of the benefits of green power may include a reduction in smog, and acid rain. Green power also minimizes financial risks. Let's face it, fossil fuels are running out and the scarcer they become, the more they are going to cost. Just go take a look at the price at your local gas station, or check out how much natural gas prices have risen lately. Green power also creates new jobs, because it tends to rely on local resources and land.

Conventional energy sources include nuclear power, coal, gas, oil, and large-scale hydropower. Green energy sources refer to power that is generated from renewable resources, such as windmills, solar power, geothermal, hydropower and biomass. Some of these are old standbys that are getting a fresh look, and some are emerging technologies. Don't worry, you don't have to understand what all those are to participate in these programs and contribute to the reduction of global warming. But in case you are interested, here's a brief primer.

 Windmills use strong winds to produce pollution free, renewable energy. In some areas, wind power is as cheap as fossil-fuel energy. The windier the location, the cheaper the energy. Solar technologies are generally more expensive, and basically convert sunlight to power. Geothermal hot water or steam from beneath the earth's surface to electricity. It creates very little pollution, and they are very economical. Biomass is crop or animal parts used to create energy and it is a very versatile fuel source.

The US Department of Energy's Energy Efficiency site listed in resources has a page where you can check what is available in your state. And there are links for more information about wind power, solar power, biomass and hydropower, should you want to learn more about any of these renewable energies.

Buy Offsets

Or, you can buy offsets. What this means is that you are paying someone to reduce or remove global warming pollution. If you want to buy 5 tons of carbon offset, the seller then guarantees that 5 fewer tons of carbon dioxide will go into the air. This is a great option for those who have already reduced their greenhouse emissions through, say, the tips in this report, but wish to do more. By buying offsets, you can get your impact down to zero, and that is a lovely number when dealing with global warming. Just think how much closer we'd be to solving the problem if everyone got their impact down to zero. The way to buy offsets is to first calculate what your impact is. You can do this on the Environmental Defense site, where you can also read about and purchase options. Then you can choose to purchase some of the offsets that most appeal to you—programs like Driving Green, which works with livestock herders in Mexico to convert livestock waste to energy. Or the Atmos Clear Club, which works with a landfill in Illinois to collect greenhouse gases from the landfill so it does not hit the atmosphere. Purchase some offsets (they generally cost from $4 to $8 per ton) and you'll be going a long, long way toward reducing your impact on the environment.

Energy Conservation Action Steps

- Turn off appliances and lights
- Adjust your thermostat
- Close your drapes at night
- Replace incandescent light bulbs with Compact Fluorescent Bulbs
- Take the CFB pledge at Environmental Defense and email it to your friends.
- Use natural daylight when possible
- Purchase green power
- Buy offsets

Water conservation

 Many people scoff at the idea that we need to conserve water. After all, it's all around us—in lakes and rivers and streams, in the rain and snow that falls from the sky. But the following statistics should help change your mind: 97% of the world's water is salty or undrinkable. 2% is locked in glaciers or ice caps. That leaves 1% of the world's water that is available for human consumption. And we need water for everything—not just our bodies, but crops and animals. We depend on it for all our needs, personal, business, manufacturing, and community. Our water supply is threatened by clear cutting of forests and runoff from industry and toxic pollution. Recent federal policies have proposed relaxing Clean Water standards—which will only make the problem worse.

According to Global Green, 1.2 billion people, or almost 1 in 5 people worldwide, are without access to safe drinking water. And, out of 191 nations in the world, 10 nations share 65% of the world's water resources. In developed countries, we take water so for granted that we let it run freely from the tap while we brush our teeth, or over-soak our yards when we carelessly forget to turn off the sprinkler. But many countries in the world don't even have the luxury of safe drinking water. It's important that we realize water is a precious resource, and its time to stop wasting it. Luckily, there are many simple things we can do.

Use Care with Storm Drains

One huge way you can make an impact on water is through various storm water programs. Have you ever considered that anything that gets washed down a storm drain goes directly to local creeks, rivers, and streams, and eventually to the ocean? Think about it—when water from your hose washes over your yard or sidewalk or driveway, it is carrying pollution along with it.

Things like fertilizer, pet waste, yard and grass clippings, paints, pesticides and motor oil can all impact our waterways through storm drains. Why is fertilizer harmful? If too much of it goes down a storm drain, it promotes the over-growth of algae in our waterways. As it decomposes, the oxygen in the water is depleted and this is harmful to water life. So don't fertilize when rain is forecast and follow instructions on the label carefully.

If you have a painting project planned, wash your brushes wisely. Do not wash them outside in the driveway, yard, or street. Instead use a basement or kitchen sink. It's not a great idea to use oil-based paint these days, but if you must, please clean your brushes in a solvent and dispose of it at a household hazardous waste collection center. Also be aware that there are green and recycled paints which we will discuss in greater detail in the "Green Home" segment.

Yard and grass clippings are unnecessary additions to our waterways and can easily be kept out of storm drains. Many communities have yard debris programs. Or consider "grasscycling" which is the practice of leaving grass clippings on the lawn after it is mowed. Don't worry—the clippings decompose rapidly, and actually return nutrients to the soil. Or start a backyard composting project—adding yard debris and grass clippings to your food waste. Many local agencies sell compost bins for very inexpensive prices. Composting is nature's way of recycling, and it's a wonderful practice that contributes to global warming prevention in several different ways.

And pet waste—ugh, just think of all the harmful bacteria and organisms in it that would reach our waterways if you allow it to go down the storm drain. We love our pets, but their waste needs to be contained. Scoop it into plastic bags and put it in the garbage.

Used motor oil needs to be properly recycled. Do not pour it down the storm drain! Every year, over 180 million gallons of motor oil are illegally dumped. That is inconsiderate to others and harmful to the planet. The same is true of pesticides, which killer creatures of all kinds in even very small doses. Look for non-toxic alternatives at your garden or home improvement store.

These are simple things you can do to prevent toxic wastes of all kinds from going in storm drains and mingling with our precious water. There are other simple water conservation tips that you can follow for your outdoor water use. Only water your lawn and garden early in the morning or in the evening. If you water during the day, in bright sunlight, most of the water is going to evaporate, rather than go into the lawn. Consider reducing the amount of lawn that you have to water in the first place—lawns take an enormous amount of water to keep them lush and green all summer. Xeriscaping or gardening with native plants is a much better way to have a beautiful yard that doesn't waste resources. Plant native or drought-tolerate species, including bushes, grasses and shrubs. Your local nursery can help you design a garden that is appropriate to your particular area.

If you do decide to stick with the lawn, install an irrigation system which will more efficiently water it. Barring that, make sure that you place your sprinklers carefully so that you are watering the yard, and not the sidewalk or street. And don't leave the water running for hours—it's not necessary for the lawn or garden and you can waste hundreds of gallons of water this way. Set at timer to remind you to turn it off if need be.

Conserve Water at Home

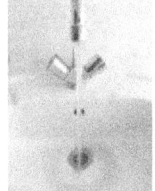 There are also many things you can do to conserve water in your daily routine. Let's start with the bathroom. Install a low-flow toilet (which can reduce waste by 20%) or a toilet dam in your toilet. What's a toilet dam? It can be something as simple as a brick or a bottle placed in your toilet tank to cut down the amount of water used with each flushing. Avoid unnecessary flushing by throwing away soiled tissues and the like in wastebaskets. Also, consider conserving by not flushing every time—if its liquid, it's okay to wait for another use. You can also

check for toilet leaks by putting food coloring in the tank. If you have a leak, color will appear in the bowl.

One of the best things you can do for your shower is to install a low-flow shower head, which can save 2.5 gallons of water a minute! An obvious suggestion is to take shorter showers. Some people turn the water on to get themselves wet, turn it off to lather up, then turn it on again to rinse. When taking a bath, fill the tub only one-third full. And remember, it actually takes far less water to take a shower than fill a bathtub. Finally, don't leave the water running when brushing your teeth, shaving, or washing your face.

There are many easy things to do in the kitchen to conserve water usage. Pour a pitcher of water, perhaps using one of the popular water filters like Brita, and put it in the refrigerator if you like your water cold. This saves you from running the water to get it cold. Along the same lines, you might consider installing one of those instant water heaters rather than running the water to get it hot.

One thing you might not have thought about is how much water an in-sink garbage disposal uses. Why not start a composting project instead? We've already learned that composting can be a great way to get rid of yard debris. And here it pops up again as an alternative to the garbage disposal. And, of course, an obvious task is to never run the dishwasher unless it is full.

When it comes to laundry, do as much of it in cold water as possible. It takes less energy all around not to have to heat the water. Your washing machine has an adjustable water level-use it. Don't waste water by running a full load with only a few items in it. There are many wonderful water-saving machines on the market these days and be aware that a front-loading machine takes less water than the traditional top-loader.

Don't be wasteful with water. Don't let it run down the drain. Whenever possible, reuse water—waste water can be used to water plants, for instance. You can also install a water recirculation device, which can save up to 16,500 gallons of water a year. That's a lot of gallons of water to save! And guess what else? This translates into cold, hard cash—to the tune of up to $50 a year.

 Don't overlook simple things, like fixing a leaky faucet. One leaky faucet can waste up to 2,700 gallons of water a year. Check the washers—most of the time it's an easy fix. If you think you have a leak, but you aren't sure here's a simple way to find out: check your water meter, don't use any water for two hours, and check it again. If the meter doesn't read the same, you've got a leak somewhere. And considering how many gallons of water you could be wasting, it's worth your while to figure out where. You can also install flow restrictors and make sure that all your pipes are well insulated.

Make Wise Food-Buying Choices

 As you can see, there are many, many actions you can take to help conserve water in your home and yard. Most of them require only minimal effort and yet create huge returns. There's another way that you can help to conserve water and that is in the choices you make in buying food. You'll find a whole section in this report about how to be a green shopper, but it is worth mentioning here, too. You see, the irrigation of agricultural crops accounts for more than 70% of freshwater consumption worldwide. That is a huge percentage, particularly in light of the fact that 1 in 5 people don't have access to safe drinkable water.

Farmers have options. They can switch to drip irrigation systems, which will result in a water savings of 30 to 70% while increasing crop yields. You have options; too—you can seek out and support local and organic farmers through the farmers markets that are  everywhere now. Farming organically has a huge impact on preventing global warming, because of the 28 most commonly used pesticides, 23 are carcinogenic and end up in our water supply. Wouldn't you rather buy and eat fresh, wholesome produce that has not been raised with toxic pesticide? Plus you'll have the added benefit of knowing that you are contributing to the health of our waterways.

Another simple thing to do is eat less meat. This may surprise you, but it takes 100 gallons of water to produce one quarter pound of meat. Yes, that burger you ate at lunch required 100 gallons of water to produce. As a comparison, one ton of beef needs 15,000 tons of water to produce; a ton of grain needs only 1,000 tons.

We'll discuss more green shopping trips later. Before we move onto giving your home a green make-over, be sure to check over the action steps below to review which activities you can instigate in your own home.

Water Conservation Action Steps

- Be careful about what you let wash down storm drains
- Recycle motor oil properly
- Buy non-toxic alternatives to pesticides
- Dispose of pet waste in the garbage
- Grasscycle your lawn
- Plant native bushes and shrubs
- Water your lawn responsibly
- Install a low-flow toilet
- Install a toilet dam
- Avoid unnecessary flushing
- Check for toilet leakage
- Install a low-flow shower head
- Take shorter showers; fill the bathtub only one-third full
- Don't leave the water running when brushing teeth or shaving
- Put drinking water in the refrigerator rather than run the tap
- Install an instant hot water heater
- Instead of using the sink disposal, compost!

- Only run the dishwasher when it is full
- Buy an energy-saving front-loading washer
- Don't let water run down the drain
- Use cold water whenever possible
- Buy a water recirculator
- Check for leaky faucets
- Install flow restrictors
- Insulate pipes
- Buy from farmer's markets
- Eat less meat

Give Your House a Green Makeover

Just as there are many things to do that contribute to water and energy conservation both indoors and out, you can also help the cause enormously by going through your home and giving it a green makeover. The Stop Global Warming website (www.stopglobalwarming.org) has a fascinating page that shares simple tips that you can do to make your house greener. The best part is that they also show the savings not only in money, but in carbon dioxide.

Start by taking a look at your water heater. What is the thermostat turned to? Make sure it's no higher than 120 degrees F. This will prevent 550 pounds of carbon dioxide from spewing into the air a year. Furthermore, it will save you around $30. Also consider

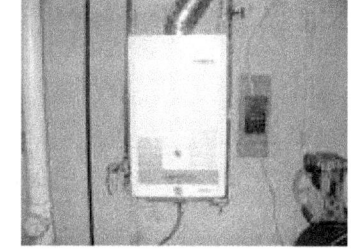

switching to a tankless water heater. This is a water heater that heats water as you use it, rather than wasting energy keeping a whole tank of water hot. Look for savings of $390 and 300 pounds of carbon dioxide. Or, simply insulate your existing water heater for a savings of 1,000 pounds of carbon dioxide and $40 per year.

Next, weatherize your home. Caulk and put weather strips on doors and windows. This can prevent 1,700 pounds of carbon dioxide and save you $274 on a yearly basis. Making sure that your walls are insulated is another smart thing to do and it can save 2,000 pounds of carbon dioxide and $245. Double pane windows prevent heat from leaking out of your home. Switching to them can save 10,000 pounds of carbon dioxide and $436 per year.

Change your air conditioning filters regularly (check your manufacturer's recommendation) and you'll see savings of $150 and 350 pounds of carbon dioxide. Or, switch to the good old-fashioned ceiling fan, which can go a long way toward cooling the air in a low-impact fashion.

Its amazing to look at all of this and see how much energy we waste, isn't it? And if that doesn't sway you, certainly looking at all those financial figures ought to. Even if you're not the least bit interested in saving carbon dioxide from spewing into the air, add up the savings of a green makeover and you'll see that there is the potential of savings thousands every year. Not bad for a few simple things to do.

One important thing to consider in giving your home a green makeover is the role appliances play. After lighting, your refrigerator and freezer are the two biggest drains on energy, and together these two appliances can be responsible for up to 8 tons of emissions per household per year.

Buy Energy Star Appliances

One of the best things you can do is to buy an energy star appliance. The Energy Star program is a joint effort between the U.S. Department of Energy and the Environmental Protection Agency. It is designed to help consumers save money while purchasing more energy efficient products.

This effort has already had a huge and successful result. In 2006, through the Energy Star program, Americans saved energy equal to the emissions of 25 million cars, and in the process saved $14 billion on their bills. Who says preventing global warming can't be cost effective?

You can participate in the Energy Star program by purchasing an Energy Star appliance. Simply look for the ones with the Energy Star labels. They have been approved by the Department of Energy and the EPA to meet stringent energy efficiency standards. There are over 50 product categories and thousands of models available.

If you are looking for a new home, look for one that meets Energy Star standards and you'll be assured you are playing your part in the fight against global warming.

Taken together, these green home makeover ideas can make a huge impact on global warming. Just think of how much we could accomplish if every person committed to making these changes. Check out the action step list below for a quick reference.

Green House Makeover Action Steps

- Turn the thermostat on your water heater down.
- Insulate your water heater
- Consider purchasing a tankless water heater
- Weatherize your home
- Check that walls are well insulated
- Install double pane windows
- Change air conditioner filters regularly
- Switch to ceiling fans
- Buy Energy Star Appliances
- If you are in the market for a new home, buy an Energy Star home

Be a Green Commuter

Ah, Americans and their cars. It's a love affair that goes back to the days of Henry Ford. But the automobile is one of the biggest offenders when it comes to global warming, and no longer can we afford to continue the same driving habits that we've always had. It's simply not good for the planet.

Scientists calculate that about half of all air pollution comes from driving cars and trucks. Every day in America, we use eight million barrels of oil in driving our cars and trucks. The average American car releases 35 pounds of carbon dioxide into the atmosphere every day. There are many alternatives to driving, such as car pooling, walking, biking, or taking mass transit, and we will discuss each option in great detail. But did you know that there are also ways that you can lessen your impact on the environment just through the way you drive, your car maintenance, and the choices you make in automobiles?

Adjust Your Driving Habits

Let's start with driving habits. First of all, drive less. Consider the following statistic: Americans drive an average of 614.5 billion miles to and from work. 614.5 billion miles. Think of the amount of carbon dioxide we are spewing into the air as we commute. Here's another statistic: according to www.hybridcars.com, since 1970, the number of vehicle miles traveled in America has increased 150 percent, while the population has increased only 40 percent. In America, there are 200 million cars, while worldwide there are 700 million.

Have you ever considered telecommuting as an alternative? With the advent of home computers and high-speed internet, this is an option that is becoming more and more feasible for a lot of people. Many professions such as writing, advertising, public relations, psychiatry, and others lend themselves to working from home. Besides being good for the environment, there are huge benefits in worker satisfaction as well. You can work in your pajamas if you choose, and take breaks when you want to. You can spend time with a child or pet as you pace yourself throughout the work day.

Even if you could telecommute just one day a week, it would make an enormous difference. According to statistics on the Environmental Defense site, if all commuters worked from home one day a week, we would save 5.85 billion gallons of oil and 143 billion pounds of carbon dioxide each year.

Another easy thing to do is group errands. Don't dash out to the store to buy milk—wait until you need other groceries, too. And better yet, wait until you have clothes to pick up at the dry cleaners (you can choose an environmentally friendly one), books at the library, and business at the bank. Then plan your route to take the most efficient way, without backtracking or traversing the city.

 How you drive can make a difference also. For starters, slow down. You might not have realized that exceeding the speed limit by even five miles per hour can result in a decrease in fuel efficiency of six percent. And, really, is that extra speed going to really get you there that much faster? How many times have you sped around a slow car on a city street only to have it catch up with you at the next stop light? As a side benefit, your stress level will be way lower. That is also true with our next tip—don't drive aggressively.

Aggressive driving is fast stops and starts, and it can be an enormous drain on your gas tank. It can lower your gas mileage by 33% on the highway and by five percent in town. We already know that driving aggressively is bad for the emotional health of you and others, so add the environment to the list. Wouldn't it be nice to actually enjoy the drive to work and home again instead of dashing about and making screeching stops?

If you are going on a road trip, travel light. For every extra 100 pounds the car carries, it reduces the fuel economy by two per cent. Also remove car carriers and bike racks when they are not in use. That will cut down wind drag and in turn boost your fuel efficiency.

Maintain Your Car for Fuel Efficiency

There are several things you can do in terms of maintaining your car that will reduce your impact on global warming. For starters, keep it tuned up. Check your engine and change oil and check spark plugs. Keeping up with routine maintenance on your car can save you up to $380 and 165 gallons of gas a year. One thing people don't realize is that your car's air filter needs changing often, and doing that one thing can make a huge difference. Changing it monthly can save 800 pounds of carbon dioxide from the air, and $130 in cash. Isn't it wonderful that there are so many options for improving the environment and saving money?

Another very simple thing to do for your car is to keep your tires inflated. Low tire pressure wastes over two million gallons of gas every day in the United States. For every pound of pressure your tires are under-inflated, fuel economy drops about one per cent. Keeping them inflated will save you a tank of gas every year—and at today's prices, that's a pretty good deal.

Buy a Hybrid

Now, suppose you've done all these things and are maintaining your car regularly, but still feel a desire to do more. You need a car to commute because mass transit is not convenient, and its' too far to ride your bike. But even with all the improvements you've made in your vehicle, you still feel guilty about how much you are driving. There are definitely a couple more options—the first is to buy a hybrid or a similar fuel efficient car and the second is to convert your car to biodiesel.

The thing about car pollution is that it tends to stick around. Scientists have calculated, for instance, that the pollution from Henry Ford's first Model T is still churning around up in the atmosphere somewhere. A household with two cars will emit 20,000 pounds of carbon dioxide into the air on a yearly basis, adding 10 tons of pollution that is going to stick around. You can begin to get the picture about why driving a fuel efficient or hybrid car is such a great option to help reduce global warming.

The first is by far the best known and the most popular. Hybrid cars have gotten enormously popular, with some brands having waiting lists to get them, although that is not as common since the $3,000 tax break is no longer available. Don't let a little matter of finances dissuade you from buying a hybrid. They are still great cars to lessen your impact on global warming.

Some popular brands of hybrids are the Toyota Prius, the Honda Accord Hybrid, the Ford Escape Hybrid, and the Lexus hybrid. In case you are confused about what a hybrid actually is, here's the deal: a hybrid combines the traditional gas-powered automobile engine with the

assistance of electricity. A car is considered a hybrid when it relies on more than one energy source. Some hybrids, such as the Prius, can run on electricity alone. These are called full hybrids. Others, such as the Chevrolet Silverado Hybrid Pick-up, can only partially utilize the electricity. These are called mild hybrids.

What essentially happens is that the electricity gives the cars a boost and they end up burning less fuel, which in turn, of course, spews less pollution into the air. The Toyota Prius, for example, switches over to the electrical system when the car is idling at a stop light. At times, the Prius burns no fuel at all. Another interesting feature of the Prius is its "regenerative brakes." These capture the thermal energy used by braking and use it for energy for other uses by the car.

Hybrid engines are also built smaller to take advantage of the fact that 99% of the time, cars does not need the extra boost to climb hills or accelerate very quickly. Hybrids use the battery to provide the extra energy that is needed for acceleration. Hybrid cars are usually also lighter to reduce wind drag and their tires are stiffer and more inflated. All in all, hybrid cars are an excellent choice for the green consumer, and more and more models are being released all the time. There are many resources available for the consumer to learn more and compare and you'll find these listed at the end of this report.

Consider Alternative Fuels

Powering cars with biodiesel or ethanol is also enjoying renewed popularity. Here's an interesting tidbit—did you know that the original Model T cars built by Henry Ford were designed to run either on gas or ethanol? That's right, the ethanol trend is not new, it's just an old idea that is being looked at with fresh eyes. What exactly is ethanol? It is a fuel made from grains and plant or animal waste. Much of today's ethanol is made from corn, and because of the surge in interest in biodiesels, corn is now being planted in record numbers to keep up with the demand.

There are benefits and downsides to biodiesel, as regards its impact on global warming. One of the biggest benefits is that biodiesel helps reduce our dependence on foreign oil, which is a huge plus right there. A group called the Agricultural Working Group wants farmers to produce 25% by 2025. Here's the deal: currently many cars can run on some kind of biodiesel, but not all can. There is a kind of ethanol called E10, which is gas blended with 10% ethanol. Many of the contemporary models of cars can run on this. Then there is E 85, which is a blend of 85% ethanol and 15% gasoline. Not quite as many cars can run on this mixture.

The downside of using biodiesel fuel is that it was not developed to prevent global warming. Thus, emissions from various biodiesels can vary enormously. And, as we learned in the section of water conservation, some agricultural practices contribute greatly to global warming and so you might not be making that big of an impact. Concerns about agriculture include the above-mentioned use of water, heavy usage of nitrogen fertilizers, which release strong emissions into the air, and plowing, which also releases toxic gases into the air. However, farmers are stewards of the earth, too, and many of them are developing better agricultural practices in order to lessen their impact on the land.

Buy a Fuel-Efficient Car

Even if you are not quite up for buying a hybrid, or converting to biodiesel, you can buy the most fuel-efficient car possible for your needs and thus do your part to prevent global warming that way. Check out the resource list at the end of this report for many links to sites that will help you discern what the most efficient car is for you. And follow a few simple guidelines to get started.

First, decide what size car you need. If you are hauling around a family of five, you might indeed need a van. Or if you are a carpenter or similar worker, you may need a truck to carry equipment and supplies. Those who enjoy a lot of camping and outdoor activities may need a SUV. But if you don't fall into any of those categories, seriously consider a smaller car. Do you really need that huge oversized SUV to drive around the city in? Why? Part of being a good citizen of the earth it taking responsibility for your choices and the impact they have on the planet. Choosing the smallest car possible is important.

Also, learn to think beyond the obvious. You may be an avid outdoor enthusiast who likes to go boating or camping and think you need a big truck or rig to haul your boat and equipment. But how many days or weeks out of the year do you actually use that truck for hauling the boat? Wouldn't it make more sense to buy a smaller, fuel-efficient car for your day to day commute and use the money you are saving on gas to rent a truck for your vacation? It also makes more sense in terms of your impact on the environment.

After you've chosen the size of vehicle you desire, look around and do some research. Then choose the most fuel-efficient and green car in the size category. Go to the yahoo green auto site (http://yahoo.com/green_center) for starters. You can also check the site at www.fueleconomy.gov for a lot of great information. The website, www.greenercars.com also has a lot of excellent independent information on green and fuel-efficient cars.

One important thing to think about when choosing a new car is to decide if you can get away with fewer add-ons. Again, do you really need four-wheel drive? If you are mostly driving in the city, the answer is no. Four-wheel drive adds a lot to fuel consumption. The same is true with super-charged, souped-up motors. There's really no need for them, and they are enormously wasteful of energy and resources. And, as we learned earlier, adding on luggage racks or bike racks to the roof of your car can make a big difference in fuel-efficiency. Take them off when you are not going to need to use them.

Clearly, there are many things you can do as a consumer to reduce your impact on the environment as you drive. You can make many simple changes with your existing vehicle, such as changing the air filter and keeping your tires inflated, and you can make changes in your driving habits like refusing to drive aggressively. One of the best things you can do is purchase a hybrid car or at least a fuel-efficient one. And, just say no to oversized trucks and SUVs unless you have good reason to use one every day. But beyond all these considerations of automobiles and driving, there are some other ways to lessen your impact on the environment. How about considering giving up your car for other alternatives?

Take Mass Transit

 These days many cities have great mass transit systems, combining buses with other alternatives such as light-rail systems. Some cities are even utilizing old-fashioned street cars and trollies, which carry people around efficiently and charmingly. And, of course, in large metropolitan areas like New York City and Washington D.C. you can utilize the subways. If you commute within a city, it can be a much better option to utilize mass transit. When you factor in the price of the gas it takes to drive your car, and things like parking, and compare it to the cost of taking mass transit, mass transit wins. Plus there are other benefits. Riding mass transit to and from work gives you time to read or think, time you wouldn't have sitting in a car, fuming about the traffic jam you are stuck in.

Most cities have aggressive programs designed to increase ridership. This will generally include websites and phone numbers you can access for information about fares and routes. You can plan ahead and eliminate any confusion you might have in advance. Mass transit is also a great option for city dwellers who are taking day trips into the city's core for shopping excursions or special events. Since parking is generally at a premium, in a city's core taking mass transit makes good sense.

As gas prices continue to rise, more and more people are taking advantage of the mass transit systems their cities offer. Ridership is up in nearly every major urban center nationwide, according to USA Today. Ridership is up 50% in Salt Lake City on their light rail system. The system has had to add more cars to accommodate the increase. Others cities such as San Francisco and Tulsa, Okalahoma are seeing people switching to mass transit in droves. It makes good sense for the pocketbook or wallet and the environment.

Another option is to pair commuting on mass transit with joining a program like Flexcar. What is a Flexcar? It is essentially a car sharing company that saves time, money and the environment. You use the cars only when you need them. You pay an hourly rate that includes gas, maintenance, and mileage. So, you get the convenience of access to a car without actually owning the car. Plus, all Flexcars are low-emission, fuel-efficient automobiles. You reserve the car by the hour, pick it up at a convenient parking location, use it, and then return it to its parking place. It's that simple. Flexcar rates are $8 per hour or $63 for the day and they are located in major cities, mostly clustered on the coasts but also including Chicago and Atlanta. You can find more locations at www.flexcar.com. Another company with similar programs is Zipcar (www.zipcar.com), which so far is offered in Chicago, London, and Vancouver.

Take Up Bike Riding

Another way to reduce your impact on the environment is to ride a bike. This not only has a major impact on how much pollution you are creating (none!), it accomplishes several other things at the same time: you'll get a great work-out from it, and you'll have fun, too.

You can ride a bike to do simple errands around town or to nearby events. Or you can take the plunge and actually bike to work. In many communities around the country, people do this every day. An excellent place for information and resources on this option is the website of the League of American Bicyclists (www.bicycleleague.org). They have compiled a whole report on bicycle-friendly cities nation-wide.

The report details what activities make each city it features bike friendly. Its platinum award winner is Davis, California, where 17% of trips to work are made by bike! The city's logo features a bicycle, and there are no school buses in town—citizens voted to get rid of them years ago, allowing children to bike or walk to school. The city has put money and resources to encouraging people to bike to work, to school, and for fun and exercise.

Many of the cities in the League's report also make it easy for bike riders to take advantage of mass transit, with easy systems for bike riders to take their bikes on buses or light rail routes. It is worth noting that May is National Bike Month, and as part of this special designation, every year there is a Bike to Work day. Local and national organizations join together to make a bicycle commute an easy, fun thing for neophytes to try. This would be a perfect day for your first bicycle commute. For more information, check www.bikemonth.com, or www.bikecommute.com. We have compiled many more resources in the listing at the end of this report.

In case you don't think bicycling to work will have much of an impact, here are some statistics from the League of American Bicyclists about bikes versus parking: the number of bikes that can fit into one car parking space ranges from six to 20! The cost of construction of one parking space in a paved lot is $2,000. It gets worse. The cost of constructing one parking space in a garage is $12,000!

Remember, too, that bicycles cost far less than an automobile to buy and maintain and you're not going to have all the additional costs of parking and the like to deal with. All in all, biking to work or for errands is a good financial and environmental decision.

Walking

In our fast-paced world, where we are so used to hopping in a car to get where we want to go, we often forget about one of the best ways to get someplace—our own two feet. Walking is great for your health  and for your mental fitness as well. It is invigorating to be outside, striding along. And, if you live within short distances of stores or libraries or other services, it can be a great way to get around.

In many major cities around the world, people use walking as their main source of transportation, and many of us grew up walking to school and sporting events. However, with the growth of suburbs and the rush of middle-class families to live there, many children of this generation live too far from school or soccer field to walk. And their parents generally live far from their workplaces, necessitating getting into the car for every errand.

This is starting to change, however. Urban planners and landscape architects are designing communities with lots of greenspace, which has been shown to boost walking and bike riding. Communities are being designed with pedestrians in mind, making some neighborhoods car-free. People are responding to these communities enthusiastically, and they have become very desirable to home buyers.

Other things you might consider is taking mass transportation part way and walking part way. Or, if you live far out of town you could drive your car part way and walk part way. This is not quite as desirable, obviously, but remember that small changes add up to a big impact. You might find you enjoy walking so much that you'll decide to move closer to your job so you can walk the whole distance.

Walking requires even less of an investment than bicycling—all you really need is a good pair of walking shoes. There are many, many websites and magazines to help you get started on choosing the correct shoes and routes and mileage, among them, www.walking.org, and www.walking.about.com. Check the resources list at the end of this report.

You might also be interested in learning more about walking by joining a walking club. There are man enthusiastic walking groups out there that you could be a part of. Joining a club not only might help you meet like-minded people, it will show you walking routes and locations you might not have known about otherwise. One walking group of interest to people who live in the New York City area is the Shorewalkers, (www.shorewalkers.org) who are dedicated to promoting and enjoying the paths and walkways along all the waters of the New York city area.

The granddaddy of all walking groups is the collection of walkers affiliated with Volksmarching. This is also sometimes called Volkswalking. The name comes from the German "Volksmarsch" which means "people's march." They are an international bunch, a group of non-competitive fitness walkers with 350 clubs that organize 3,000 events yearly. For events and club info in the United States, check www.ava.org, for more information. In Canada, you'll want to go to www.walks.ca to learn more.

There are so many different ways to become a green commuter, it's practically a crime not to implement some of them, and they are so easy and effective. And, as we are learning repeatedly, small steps can add up to big results. Make a commitment to becoming a green commuter today, and then choose one of several of the above-mentioned options and you will know you are making a positive impact to the problem of global warming.

Green Commuter Action Steps
- Drive less
- Telecommute

- Drive more slowly
- Don't drive aggressively
- Group errands
- Travel light
- Keep your auto tuned up
- Check air filters monthly
- Check tire pressure
- Look into biodiesel
- Buy a hybrid
- Buy a fuel-efficient car
- Take mass transit
- Take Up Bike Riding
- Walk!
- Join a Volksmarching club

Be Green at Work

You may have worked very hard to makeover your home into a green dream, and have implemented strategies for environmentally-minded commuting. But then one day you pull up to work on your bike, park it, and take a look around. The thought occurs to you that your workplace has one heap of a long ways to go to make a difference in its environmental impact. Never fear, we can help. Whether you are an employee or the boss, you can make a huge difference in the environmental health of your workplace. And guess what? Greening the office has a positive impact on employee morale and the bottom line, too.

Recycle

 An easy way to have a big impact at work is to recycle. We'll discuss recycling in depth in the next section of this report, and you'll find many, many resources at the end of this report that can give you more information. But for starters, be aware that recycling at work is easy to set up and simple to implement. It doesn't take much extra personal effort or energy at all to separate out paper into a special recycling bin for instance. And setting up bins for glass and plastic in the lunchroom can have a big impact.

An integral part of a work recycling program is using green materials. Use recycled paper and products that have been processed in eco-friendly ways. The key to buying good recycled paper is to choose papers with a high post-consumer waste ratio. Many people aren't aware of this, but even recycled paper uses an enormous amount of energy in its processing, and a lot of chemicals too. One thing the industry would rather not have you know is that it often uses toxic pulp slurry in its processing. Avoid all this by buying high post-consumer waste content recycled paper. Also, write on both sides of the paper. Choose printers that will easily print on two sides of the paper. If this is not possible, then utilize the backsides of printed papers for notes or to-do lists.

Even materials such as pens and pencils can be made from recycled materials, and you can buy refillable pens and pencils. And what about using biodegradable soaps in the bathroom and for cleaning? Also try to use cloth towels to replace paper towels as much as possible.

Embrace the Paper-less Office

Remember a few years back all the brouhaha about the paperless office? Despite all the hype, and despite the fact that every office is now computerized, the paperless office is still a long ways away. However, that doesn't mean we have to give in to the urge to use so much paper. Digitize as much as possible. "The greenest paper is no paper at all," says the folk at Treehugger (www.treehugger.com). Look at documents online instead of printing them out, and send email wherever possible. Keep files on computers and make backups with CDs or zip discs. You can even get software called Greenprint www.printgreener.com , which takes out blank pages and other wasteful filler from documents before printing. The software lets you see what the file contains, click on what you want to print and delete what you don't want. For instance, if you are printing a few pages from a website that are full of ads and extraneous material, you can choose to print only the relevant information. This saves not only paper and trees, but ink cartridges and wear and tear on your computer as well. There's also a feature which sends the document straight to a pdf file, eliminating the need to print at all.

The folks who brought you Greenprint have also recently launched a new product that is equally exciting. It is called EverGreen, which saves paper by maximizing the number of words per page, without destroying readability. The company says that compared to Ariel and Times New Roman, EverGreen reduces paper use by 15 to 20%. Consider this: there are 3.2 billion reams of office paper used in the United States each year alone. Even a 15% reduction would have a significant impact. Changing fonts to achieve such a monumental reduction has to be one of the easiest of activities around.

Check Energy Saving Settings on the Computer

Okay, so you've realized that it's not a good idea to put your computer to sleep at night, because that is just draining energy for no good reason, right? But did you also realize that some computers and office equipment have settings that drain power even when they are turned off but still plugged in? For starters, switch your computers to their energy saving modes and be sure to turn them off at night, don't just put them on standby. To make sure that computers, and monitors, printers, televisions, etc., are truly not drawing power, you need to pull the plug. Or a better option may be to simply use a power strip. Then with one simple switch you can turn everything off completely. If you think the power that would be saved in this way would be so insubstantial as to not be worth it, think again. In 2002, Low Power Model Energy (sometimes called lopomo) was responsible for 10% of the power usage in California homes. So pull those plugs and flip those power switches when you leave for home at night.

Use Reusables

Like so many of us, you may enjoy a coffee habit. Perhaps you sip coffee throughout the day as you work, or go to a local coffee shop for a break in the morning or afternoon. Many offices and coffee shops use paper or Styrofoam cups for ease, but don't fall  into this habit. Bring a favorite mug from home to use for your coffee at work and encourage your co-workers to do the same. Or, lobby your boss to buy a set of coffee mugs for everyone in the office. One idea is to buy handmade ceramic mugs from local artisans, thus encouraging a handmade esthetic.

Don't stop with the office. You can take your mug into Starbucks or any other coffee shop and have them fill it with your favorite latte or cappuccino. Most specialty coffee chains also sell insulated travel mugs for coffee, some of which are specially designed to fit in a beverage holder in your car (although that won't be necessary, since you are finding alternative ways to commute). These reusable mugs and cups are so much more eco-friendly and way more pleasant to drink from, also.

Then, too, it's important not just to stop with your coffee. Think about your lunch choices. Bringing your lunch to work in reusuable containers is a much better option than going for take out, which is likely to be given to you in Styrofoam or plastic containers, which lots of extra waste products included. Think of the last time you bought fast food, and how many extra napkins, ketchup packets and small containers of salt were thrown in. All this excess adds up—and not just on our waistlines.

Buy Carbon Offsets for Business Travel

Earlier in this report, we talked about buying offsets to make up for the amount of carbon you personally are responsible for producing. Did it occur to you to buy them to make up for business travel also? Better yet, have your employer buy them—for you and all other employees. Include air and car travel when calculating how much carbon you are responsible for and how much carbon offsets to buy. Several sites can help you calculate what your impact is and how much to buy to offset it. At www.itm.org.uk the Icarus Toolkit will help corporate travel managers why, what, and how to measure carbon emissions. It also lists corporate green travel guidelines and informs about how to implement a green travel program. For easy reference there are case studies of several corporations and what they did to implement a program.

Create Green Commuting Programs

You've committed to be a green commuter, now its time to get all those folks you work with in on the act. Organize carpools for employees who live in similar areas. Or organize a group bike commute? How about meeting someone who lives close by and taking the bus together? There's power in numbers, and sometimes it is easier and more fun to do something in tandem or a group than alone. Better yet, consider….

Telecommuting

We discussed this briefly in a previous section of this report, but it's worth mentioning again. Did you know that over 44 million Americans now telecommute? They've discovered the joys of working from home. With the internet, instant messaging, video and phone conferencing and other tools, it's easier than ever to accomplish telecommuting. Many companies are seeing a positive impact not only on employee morale but on the bottom line, and are allowing more and more employees to work from home. Talk to your boss—he or she may be surprisingly open to the idea. Start small, working from home one day a week, and then build. You will love the freedom and flexibility that working from home gives you.

Green up the Building You Work In

Finally, don't overlook giving your physical surroundings a green makeover.   Start with your office furniture, which can also be made from recycled materials, as can lighting. For instance, you can choose high-end LED lamps that use very small amounts of energy. And consider relying on natural daylight as much as possible—it's been proven to boost employee moral. Think about the air you breathe at the office. Good circulation is crucial, as anyone who has ever gotten the same cold multiple times as it is passed through the office. Good ventilation is important.

Now, what about the building itself? Did you know that buildings account for 30% of all carbon emissions? That's a pretty hefty percentage. But there are ways to minimize this. Some buildings use solar panels to cut down reliance on fossil fuels and electricity.   Green roofs and greywater programs are also very popular. Insist on installing low-flow toilets

Under the auspices of the U.S. Green Building Council, LEED operates. What is LEED? It is the Leadership in Energy and Environmental Design and it oversees a Green Building Rating system for both new construction and existing buildings. The LEED rating system is considered to be the national benchmark "design, construction, and operation of high performing green buildings." LEED focuses its attention on five main areas: sustainable site development, water savings, energy efficiency, materials selection and indoor environmental quality.

LEED has many programs and educational systems at all levels to help you learn how to make your existing building greener or build a new one that meets their standards. LEED has guidelines for schools, retail and campuses, also. It's a very comprehensive program that will assist you in making all kinds of decisions and plans for your green building, no matter where you are at now. Access their site at www.usgbc.org.

Another organization that is working on green building initiative is Global Green (www.globalgreen.org) which we have already mentioned. This group works in partnership with local governments and other public entities to "demonstrate the benefits of green building, outline options for establishing green building programs that protect local quality of life and the environment, provide training for staff and constituents, and encourage the development of incentives for green building projects." The group has partnered already with many cities in California, including Los Angeles, Santa Monica, San Francisco and San Jose.

The organization has published a step-by-step guidebook for local governments that will help them to develop their own green building programs. You'll also find all kinds of links to information and other resources for green building at their site. It's worth a look.

You can see that there are many, many ways to get your workplace on a greener footing, and also to get fellow employees on board. Some ideas are so simple you won't have any trouble convincing others to go along. Others may be a little more difficult to implement, but once people start seeing results, they will want to go along.

Green at Work Action Steps

- Recycle
- Use Green Materials
- Say hello to the paper-less office
- Check energy-saving settings on computers and peripherals
- Pull the plug!
- Use reusables

- Buy carbon offsets for business travel
- Telecommute
- Green up your building's interior
- Look into the LEED certification program

Recycling

Recycling is probably the first thing people think of when they hear about global warming and want to do something to make a difference. This is good. Recycling can make a huge difference in the quality of our lives and we'll share some statistics and facts with you to prove it. Please bear in mind, though, that there is much more that you can do than just recycle. Some people think that because they are recycling a few cans and bottles they are doing their share. Nothing could be further from the truth. Everyone needs to recycle, true; everyone also needs to take some of the many other steps we have detailed in this report.

Here's why everyone needs to be a conscious recycler: in 2005, 492 billion pounds or 246 million tons of municipal waste was created in the United States. On a bright note, 30% of that waste was recycled or composted into new products. Those figures are way up from 1980, when only 9.6% of waste was recycled or composted. In general, recycling lessens the need to extract raw materials from the planet. So does buying recycled materials. For instance, it can take 20 times more energy to create an aluminum can from raw ore than it does to create it from recycled aluminum.

Okay, now to get you up to date on the latest status of recycling. What, exactly is recycling? Wikipedia defines it as "the reprocessing of materials into new products." Simple enough, right? And it is, if we all do it. An easy way to remember the guidelines of recycling are to follow the three Rs: Reduce, Reuse, and Recycle. To begin with, it's important to minimize your garbage by choosing products with minimal packaging, composting, and being a conscious consumer. We will talk more about this in the section on shopping that follows. It's also a good idea to reuse items as much as possible. One good rule of thumb is to try to reuse everything at least once before turning it into recycling. For instance, use the plastic bag you brought your groceries home in as storage in the refrigerator before you recycle it. Or see if you can't find a use for that glass bottle in some way.

Recycling Household Items

The problem is that we can't always find second uses for our consumer products. Which is where recycling comes in. Nearly every major city in America now has a curbside recycling center, and these  programs have become so simple they are a breeze to use. In many cities, red or yellow recycling buckets are ubiquitous. However, more and more cities are switching over to the use of one roll cart for all recycling needs. Every city will have slightly different guidelines for how to prepare recyclables, so in general, it is a good idea to check with your local government or garbage hauler to learn more.

If your city is one that does not have curbside recycling, it will at least have drop-off location. If you are not sure where to take recyclables, check in with the Earth 911 website (www.earth911.org) which has a locator page. All you have to do is put your state and zip code in and it will connect you with the information you need.

 So, what household waste can be recycled? In general, you can recycle plastics, glass, steel, aluminum cans and foil, and paper. These days, most plastics can be recycled. There's one catch: different kinds of plastic cannot be mixed in the recycling process. Even a small amount of the wrong kind of plastic can ruin a batch of melting recycling. The average consumer cannot tell the difference in types just by sight or touch and so the plastic industry has responded with a system of marking and numerical grades. These are generally found on the bottom of the container. Please note that just because a plastic container has a coded number on it, it does not mean that it can be recycled. Nor does it mean that the container has recycled material in it. While not all curbside programs will take all plastics, you can probably find a drop-off location that will take them, also.

As for the plastic bags you bring your groceries home in, world-wide one trillion of them are used every year. That figure alone ought to have you choosing paper. While some studies have shown that paper bags take as much energy to produce as plastic, many people end up reusing the paper bags to separate their recycling into at the curbside. However, the very best option is to buy cloth bags and take your own to the store and reuse them over and over. Many retail stores have become aware of this, and are starting to charge customers for plastic bags. At the same time, they are giving customers a small discount if they bring in cloth bags. The furnishing giant IKEA recently announced it would be charging customers a nickel per plastic bag, and at the same time, it is lowering the price on its reusable bags from 99 to 59 cents. IKEA plans to eventually phase the plastic bags out. After all, they go through an average of 70 million plastic bags a year in the US alone.

Otherwise, nearly all aluminum cans, foil, and bottles are taken in most recycling programs. It is good to know that it is no longer necessary to remove labels on cans or bottles for recycling purposes. As far as rinsing, sometimes it can be difficult to get food residue out without wasting a lot of water. The latest recommendations are to simply rinse enough to get obvious food remnants and odors out and don't worry about the rest.

Of course, most all of us know that nearly every kind of paper can be recycled, from newspapers to office and computer paper. Earlier, we discussed the importance of buying post-consumer waste recycled paper. What kinds of paper products cannot be recycled? Those contaminated with food waste, waxed paper, waxed cardboard milk and juice containers, carbon paper, and pet food bags and laminated paper. Use your good judgment on this.

Don't forget to recycle ink cartridges from your printer also. Many companies have simple recycling processes that make it very easy to do. HP, for example, includes a pre-paid envelope in which to recycle the old cartridge with every ink cartridge purchase. All the consumer has to do is put the cartridge in the envelope and drop it in a mailbox. It couldn't be easier.

Recycling Batteries

 One of the things it might not occur to you to recycle is batteries. We use batteries for laptops, Ipods, calculators, you name it. Batteries are part and parcel of our busy, on the go, connected lives. Batteries are comprised of heavy metals, and in some cases, toxic metals like cadmium, mercury, alkaline, lead acid, and nickel metal hydride. Some of the problems batteries can cause when improperly disposed of include, polluting of waterways due metals vaporizing into the air when they are burned; exposing the environment to metals and leads; contain strong corrosive acids and burn the skin if exposed to these acids.

Batteries that end up in landfills and incinerators leak into the environment and cause all kinds of problems like the ones detailed above. In 1996, the government created the Battery Act. This law addressed the problem of mercury in batteries, and put in place a system to phase it out and it provided for the creation of recycling programs for batteries. There are several different types of batteries, and each one requires different disposal methods.

In general, it's a good idea to check with your local governments and facilities to learn where and how you can recycle household batteries. Alkaline batteries used to have a great deal of mercury in them and as such were not allowed in landfills or incinerators, but since the passage of the battery act, these batteries tend to have far less mercury and are now allowed again. Nickel Metal Hydride batteries are commonly used in laptops and can be recycled. Nickel Cadmium batteries are commonly known as rechargeable batteries. They are considered hazardous waste and must be recycled. Button cell batteries used in watches, calculators, hearing aids and other small devices contain silver and mercury. These are hazardous waste and must be recycled. One of the other helpful results of the 1996 Battery Act is that batteries are now labeled "battery must be recycled" if such is the case.

You can follow a few simple guidelines to choose batteries. First of all, read labels. With the onset of the Battery Act, much of the mercury in batteries has been reduced. But read labels to make sure you know what you are buying. Always choose brands that have fewer heavy and toxic metals.

Consider not using rechargeables. Yes, it's true they do fall into the category of reusables. This, in turn, results in a longer life and less frequent need to buy batteries. However, and this is a big however, rechargeable batteries still contain heavy metals such as nickel cadmium. While using rechargeable batteries does decrease the number of batteries entering the waste stream, it increases the potential for heavy metal toxins to be released into the atmosphere if they aren't recycled properly. Always, always recycle them.

Cell Phones

Cellular telephones are enormously popular world-wide these days. With manufacturers constantly coming out with new and better models and versions, consumers are tempted to buy replacements for their old phones more and more often. One environmental research firm estimates that consumers now replace their cell phones on average of once every 18 months. With 128 million Americans using cell phones as long ago as 2001, that adds up to a lot of cell phones in the waste stream. This same group estimates that 130 million cell phones were disposed of in 2005. Because so many of us don't know what to do with old cell phones, we end up storing them in a closet at home. This means that soon there will be up to 500 million cell phones in need of disposal.

And, consumers who suspect that it's not a good idea to just toss them out are correct. Cell phones contain lead and mercury and these toxic wastes could be released into the atmosphere if we consign our phones to the landfill.

Luckily, many organizations and groups have created plans for the recycling or donation of cell phones. There is likely one in your area. Check the Earth 911 (www.earth911.org) website to find a nearby group that can help you.

Paint

We even have to worry about paint now? Yes, indeed we do. Anyone who has ever completed a painting project knows how easy it is to overestimate the amount of paint you will need. Odds are good you have leftover buckets of paint sitting in your garage or basement right now. Oil-based paints and thinners have hazardous waste in them. Water-based paints do not, but our over eagerness for home improvement projects means that landfills get inundated with paint cans.

Amazingly enough, the National Paint and Coating Association says that the equivalent of two cans of paint is sold for each American every year. The best way to minimize the impact of a painting project on the environment is to plan carefully and don't over buy. Buy only what you need. Paint stores and websites offer calculators to figure your needs. Just keep painting—continue the project until the paint is gone. If you have a little bit too much, put it on the walls. You'll get a longer-lasting paint job and the satisfaction of knowing that you've kept paint out of the landfill. Or, use leftover paint for another project, or as a primer for another project.

Some communities have reuse or recycling programs for paint. Recycling programs collect paint from businesses or homes and actually reprocess it into new paint. Be aware also that not all communities accept the steel paint cans themselves for recycling. Again, the best bet is to call.

Christmas Trees

More and more consumers are moving to buy artificial trees for the holidays. Many might think they are being environmental in making this choice—after all, you can reuse an artificial tree year after year, season after season. But, that is not necessarily true. Artificial trees are a  petroleum-based product. They contain non-degradable plastics and some have toxic lead or metals in them. Artificial trees contain poly vinyl chloride, or PVC, and that is one of the worst offenders when it comes to environmental toxins, because it contains lead. They only retain their looks for a few years, after which they will need to be tossed out, and the plastics and toxins they contain only add to the problem of emissions and overused landfills. An artificial tree consigned to landfill will not biodegrade—it will sit there for centuries.

Real Christmas trees are a renewable, recyclable resource. Current statistics say there 500,000 acres of Christmas trees growing in America. Each of these acres produces oxygen for 18 people.   This means that the Christmas trees growing in the United States today create oxygen for 9 million people! Trees are an important part of the fight against global warming, because they take carbon dioxide out of the air and replace it with oxygen.

 Christmas trees can be grown on soil that doesn't support other crops, and Christmas tree farms are a renewable resource, with most growers planting 3 seedlings for every 1 tree they harvest. As discussed earlier, it is important to buy local whenever possible. Support a local tree farmer if you live in an area where trees are grown.

The website of the National Christmas Tree Association (www.christmastree.org) lists a variety of ways that people around the country and the world are using recycled Christmas trees to benefit the environment. For instance, a pharmaceutical company in Toronto, Canada, plans to make an influenza medicine with an acid extracted from the needles of recycled Christmas trees. In Indiana, volunteers gathered trees and distributed them on a 25-acre wildlife rehabilitation site. The trees will provide cover for chipmunks, birds, raccoons, and all kinds of small animal, protecting them from predators and giving them shelter in harsh weather. Recycle Christmas trees have been used for dune restoration in Gulf Shores, Alabama and for marsh reclamation in Louisiana. In Wisconsin, recycled trees are used as energy to power a pulp and paper mill. It's amazing how many creative uses there are for natural products such as Christmas trees.

The most common use for discarded Christmas trees is to turn them into mulch. A program in allows residents to recycle their Christmas trees either curbside or at drop-off locations. The resulting mulch is then offered to residents for free. A program in Georgia has recycled 4 million trees into mulch.

As you can see, there are many creative ways to recycle Christmas trees. Most cities have extensive tree recycling programs, with drop-off locations and curbside pick-up common. Often boy scouts run programs as a fundraiser, offering to pick up your tree for a nominal charge. You can check on the Earth 911 website (www.earth911.org) or at the National Christmas Tree Association (www.christmastree.org) for more information on programs and to find the location of a recycler in your area.

Composting

Along the same lines of recycling Christmas trees, have you ever considered composting? What is composting? It is organic matter that can be used as a soil amendment or to grow plants. Anyone who has ever used compost in a garden bed knows that it creates superior soil in which plants will flourish. It can also be used as mulch, and is an excellent alternative to commercial fertilizers. It loosens clay soils and also aerates all types of soils and increases their capacity to hold water. Compost contains microorganisms, which keeps the soil in a balanced condition. All these reasons are why plants love it!

Composting is not only good for your garden; it can make a huge contribution to global warming. Almost all organic material is compostable, and keeping as much out waste of our landfills as possible is one way to contribute to a green environment. Don't  throw it away—compost it. Many people are accustomed to putting organic material such as food waste down the in-sink garbage disposal. But disposals use an incredible amount of water and some electricity to accomplish their job. It's much better to simple toss food waste into a bucket beside your garbage can and add it to the compost pile.

You may be surprised at how much recycling your food waste can reduce your garbage, too. These days, more and more cities are either refusing to pick up yard debris, or asking you to separate it into special bags or garbage cans. Since you are separating it out anyway you might as well separate it into a compost pile.

The compost decomposition process mimics what nature does on the forest floor or in other natural areas. Plants and leaves die, fall to the ground and remain there, where they slowly decompose. Organisms in the soil feed on them and break them down and eventually they become part of the forest or jungle floor. Just like the forest floor, your compost pile will have millions of tiny organism working hard for you in it. Some of these will be bacteria, fungi, worms and insects. Some are visible to our eyes, and some are so tiny that they aren't. It's a whole active magical world beneath the soil.

How to make compost? There are many, many websites which can help you get started, so be sure to check the resources list at the end of this report. There are also many online stores that can sell you composting equipment, including bins for the compost itself and containers to put your food waste in. However, the truth of the matter is that all you really need for compost is an area in which to pile waste. Most people like to make compost in a hidden area, or confine it to a bin, but, no matter, what—compost happens. It's a natural biological process.

You can get as complicated or as simple as you want with compost but the bottom line is that it's going to be a benefit to your garden and society, so why not start out quickly and easily? The Compost Guide site (www.compostguide.com) has a page with a step by step guide to get a compost pile quickly and easily. They recommend starting with a larger pile, up to three feet by three feet and combining yard debris with food waste. A larger pile generates more heat, and heat is what gets a compost pile decomposing. It's important to keep the pile aerated by turning it frequently, and find the correct balance for wetting it down. A compost pile needs to be damp but not too wet. Keep a balanced mixture of green and brown materials. In other words, don't put too much yard debris or too much food waste—either can unbalance the compost.

What all can go into a compost pile? The idea is to mix "browns," which are carbon-rich materials such as wood chips, straw, and dried leaves, with "greens" which are green leaves, grass clippings and kitchen scraps. The basic ratio is 25 parts brown to 1 part greens, but the beauty and fun of compost is that it is not an exact science, more of an art that you will learn by trial and error.

You can add to your compost pile grass clippings, leaves (if you have a chipper, grind them up for quicker decomposing), pine needles, wood ashes and garden refuse. Almost all kitchen waste can be added with a few exceptions. Meat will take a long time to break down and may create odors and attract flies. Egg shells also rot slowly, so break them up before adding them. High-fat foods like salad dressings and peanut butter may also attract insects so be wary. When you add the kitchen waste to your compost pile, cover it with about 8 inches of brown material which will help to keep insects and other pests away.

You can have a passive or a managed pile. A passive pile means you just pile it up and let it rot. A managed pile means you will be turning it to aerate it, watering it sometimes, and constantly adding new materials. You may want to check the internal temperature of the pile, making certain it is hotter than the outside air, in order to get the quickest results. If you pay a lot of attention to a managed pile, you may have new compost within 3 to 4 weeks.

Composting is a wonderful activity for families and children, too—it's a great way to teach kids about the wonders of the natural world. An added bonus is that the end result helps on a micro and macro level. Compost enriches our gardens and contributes to the prevention of global warming.

Recycled Clothing

Last, but not least, think about your wardrobe and begin to look at creative ways to recycle clothing. There's been a huge surge in popularity in do it yourself projects lately, and the internet is filled with sites that teach sewing and knitting and other crafts. A popular sub-set of this is using recycled materials for these crafts. Some knitters visit thrift stores and buy old wool sweaters, then unwind them and use the wool for new projects. Many creative sewers buy old sweaters and clothing, cut them apart and reassemble them into fashionable creations. Some times wool sweaters are thrown in the washing machine and felted, then made into purses or blankets or hats. There are many, many creative ways to re-make old clothing. Some crafty creators host parties where they swap their thrift store finds and share ideas for making new items from old.

And don't turn up your nose at shopping thrift stores for apparel to use as is. Many, many thrift shops get donations from specialty stores and sometimes just from women clearing out their closets. There are also many wonderful re-sale shops sprouting up, where someone else's discarded outfit can become your new favorite thing to wear. Our ancestors knew all about recycling clothing. They cut down one child's dress to fit the younger ones coming up, and when they'd gotten as much wear as possible, they cut it into scraps to be used in patchwork quilts. Much of the time, they had no way to buy more, limited either by availability or money. These quilts are considered stunning works of art today—and they were all created out of the necessity to recycle clothing and use every bit of fabric on hand.

If you lack the time or inclination to be crafty yourself, never fear, you can buy recycled clothing. Look around on the internet and you'll find many small companies that sell unique recycled clothing and accessories. At Escama (www.escama.com) you can buy elegant handbags made from 100% post-consumer recycled aluminum—flip-top tabs. These bags are fashioned in Brazil by two cooperatives of women artisans, and so their purchase is also helping them to earn a decent living. At Recycle Bin (www.recycledbindesigns.com) you'll find clothing made from recycled items with a hippie esthetic. RetroActif Designs (www.retroactif.com) makes wonderful handbags and totes from recycled artist's banners.

The good people at Treehugger (www.treehugger.com) have compiled a large section on recycled and green fashion, with numerous links to small retailers and many articles.

Also look here for fashionable tote bags to take to the store for groceries and other items. Once you start looking around, you'll be amazed at the great variety of stylish options for recycled clothing.

On a somewhat related vein, an entry on the Green Options blog (www.greenoptions.com) talks about recycled art. Megan Prusynski talks about how artists have a long history leading the change that is necessary in society. She sites artist Andy Goldsworthy as an example of an artist who makes are with natural materials in a natural setting. The artist Marcel Duchamp took found objects and made them into art in the early 1990s. For much intriguing information on green art and green artists, visit the Green Museum (www.greenmusem.org).

You can see that the subject of recycling is large and includes many different areas. And, it is vital to the prevention of global warming that all of us do all that we can to reduce, reuse, and recycle as much as possible. As awareness about this grows, more and more programs are starting up that make it easier for the consumer to recycle.

Recycling Action Steps

- Follow the three Rs: Reduce, Reuse, Recycle
- Recycle household items
- Find a drop-off location if necessary
- Recycle batteries
- Recycle or donate cell phones
- Calculate painting projects carefully
- Buy a real Christmas tree and recycle it
- Start a compost pile
- Wear recycled clothing
- Craft your own recycled wardrobe

Shop Green

 Consumers have many options available to them to show their support for the green industry. You can essentially vote with your pocketbook, saying yes to green vendors and manufacturers and farmers who practice wise stewardship of resources. You can choose to buy local, patronizing farmers markets and shopping at stores owned my local companies. And you can make many simple choices such as carrying groceries in reusable totes and shunning products with a lot of excess packaging. There are also many choices for biodegradable cleaning and fashion and beauty products that are less harmful to our planet.

You can make an impact without even changing your usual shopping habits by much. We've already discussed how many plastic bags end up in landfills, and talked about the wisdom of choosing paper bags (and recycling them) or, better yet, buying cloth tote bags that can be reused over and over. But you can make a difference in other simple ways also.

One-third of all industrial waste in the United States comes from product packaging. And get this—for every dollar that we spend on cereal, only 9cents of that actually goes for the cereal. The other 91 cents is all spent on the packaging and advertising. The way to combat this is to grocery shop with the three Rs in mind. As a refresher, the three Rs are: Reduce, Reuse, and Recycle.

First of all, reduce. Ironically, with grocery shopping, this sometimes means going bigger and buying larger sizes, which will result in less packaging. Buying bigger containers of cereal means you aren't donating quite so much to the packaging and advertising side of things. And, consider buying in bulk, which saves money and packaging and will often provide you with quality natural products you might not find elsewhere. Choose products that don't have a lot of excess packaging, and if you must buy something with an extra box around it, be sure to recycle that. Minimize the plastic bags you choose when picking produce, too. You can buy many products, such as apples and avocados, loose.

Next, reuse. Buy groceries in reusable containers. Don't buy single serving items such as Lunchables and puddings or small containers of carrots. These things are very convenient, yes, but how difficult is it for you to buy bigger packages and put them into reusable containers yourself? Buy juices in concentrates and mix them in your own pitchers. (Remember, waxed juice containers are not recyclable.)

Finally, recycle. We learned all about recycling in the last section. And it is important to reiterate that recycling is not the answer to all our problems. The danger is that people think if they recycle a few glass items they've done their part. Nothing could be further from the truth. It's equally important to prevent waste before we buy it.

Remember that the third R, recycle, also includes buying recycled material, such as printer paper. Look for packaging that is recycled also.

Even though we learned how wonderful recycling is, you can reduce much of your food waste by planning ahead. Buy what you will eat before it spoils. Take advantage of your freezer space. Eat leftovers, and learn to be creative with them in meals. Many top chefs and bakers know the value of using leftovers, turning day-old pastries into bread puddings and creating soups from leftover vegetables. You can follow their lead.

One problem is the serving sizes you will find at many restaurants these days. There are creative ways to get around this. Consider sharing a meal with a dining companion. Or take home your leftovers in a doggie bag—and if the restaurant brings you a Styrofoam or plastic container, be sure to tell them that paper containers work just as well and are more environmentally friendly.

Another thing you can do is eat less meat. Earlier we discussed how many resources meat production consumes. As a reminder, 100 gallons of water is used for every quarter pound of meat. That amount of meat is what many people consume for lunch or dinner every day, so multiplied millions of times over, you can see what an impact this has. One ton of beef requires 15,000 tons of water to produce.

Shop at Farmer's Markets

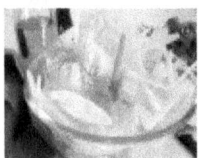 Organic and locally grown produce has become so popular, it is the rare city that doesn't now have a variety of farmer's markets and most have several. While most people choose farmer's markets for the delicious variety of produce available, did you know that shopping there has a huge impact on the environment? Well, it does. That is because that much of the produce we buy at the supermarket is either trucked over thousands of miles or flown in from distance countries. We are now used to buying strawberries in the dead of winter, but did you ever stop to consider how much energy is consumed to give you that luxury? Those berries are no doubt grown far away, in the southern hemisphere where the seasons are reversed. They then have to be flown on a jet to the United States, using jet fuel and other resources.

Shopping at a farmer's market bypasses these problems. You support local farmers and buy food that is delicious and full of nutrition, often even grown organically. And don't forget that most farmers' markets also feature booths with fresh-caught fish (if you live on a coast), organic eggs, homemade cheeses, honeys, and other wonderful delicacies. A few simple tips: take your own bags (again, why load up on plastic?) and take cash. Don't be afraid to talk to the farmers to learn about their practices. Also be aware that it is an expensive and time-consuming process to get certified organic and some small producers may use organic processes but simply not have had time to get certified.

To find farmer's markets in your area, visit, www.farmersmarkets.com and or the USDA's directory to farmers markets (www.ams.usda.gov).

Recently, many people have taken up the cause of eating locally, with bloggers and families challenging themselves to eat only local for a certain period of time. You can take the Eat Local challenge yourself and learn much more about the movement at www.eatlocal.net. Besides farmer's markets, other ways to eat local include buying from local grocers and co-ops, joining a community supported agriculture program, which will deliver organic produce to you weekly, and preserve food when it is ripe for later use. The website also talks about ways to preserve foods and has many interesting tips on produce (such as, 97% of vegetable varieties grown in 1900 are now extinct).

The Eat Local challenge site provides a scorecard you can fill out and send in. They advise that taking the challenge in the summer months, when local produce is abundant, is the easiest route, but if you really want to challenge yourself, do it in December! The basic guidelines are these: spend 10% of your grocery budget on local food (which is defined as grown within a one-hundred mile radius); try one new fruit or vegetable each day; and preserve food to enjoy later in the year.

Several books have recently been released with eating local and the challenges therein as the theme. Look for them wherever bookstores are sold or on Amazon or Barnes and Noble or Abe Books online. In, *Animal, Vegetable, Miracle*, the novelist Barbara Kingsolver writes about her year of eating locally and provides much information about the environment as well as recipes along the way. Another book is called *Plenty,* by Alisa Smith and J.B. MacKinnon, and it is on the same subject from a slightly different angle. Both shed a lot of light on the Eat Local movement, as well as inspiration for those who want to try it themselves.

Green Cleaning

 Have you ever considered that it might be time to rethink how you clean your home? The cleaning products that we have grown used to purchasing and using may have hidden toxins in them. It's also time to review our cleaning procedures, thinking about reducing our dependence on paper towels, for instance.

Deidre Imus, in her book, *Green This! Volume 1: Greening Your Cleaning,* writes about the dangers of toxins in our commercial cleaning products. She says there has not been enough long-term testing of some ingredients in these products to determine their impact not only on the environment but on the people who live in our homes. And she says that ingredients in many common household cleaners have been linked to childhood cancers. Clearly, it is time for us to take a look at our cleaning products.

According to the Environmental Protection Agency, levels of toxins inside the home can be from 2 to 100 percent higher than outside (and  we have already seen how many emissions we are spewing into the air). Where do these toxic levels come from? Decorating and cleaning products. But consumers need to be aware of the various issues around labeling and choose wisely. For instance, the word "natural" on a product is undefined and unregulated by the government—and thus means nothing. Someone could create a toxic mixture and slap the word "natural" on it and nobody would stop them. No standards exist for terms such as "non-toxic" or "eco-safe" or "environmentally friendly," either.

What's a consumer to do? Go to www.eco-labels.org website where you will find much information and also a label report card where you can look for specific information on your products. There are also helpful articles.

You can also buy environmentally friendly cleaning products. One brand that gets consistently high rankings from environmentalists is Seventh Generation, which has household and personal care products that are safe for the environment and people. The company also has a new book out, *Naturally Clean,* by Jeffrey Hollander and Geoff Davis, that explains the dangers of traditional cleaning products. The book analyzes over 300 natural and traditional cleaners.

Other companies that are known for creating good green product lines are Mrs. Meyers (www.mrsmeyers.com) and Shaklee (www.shaklee.com).

Don't forget, also to check out your personal care and beauty products. You can find out more about Eco-labels. Many cosmetic lines include chemicals that you probably don't really want on or near your skin. The family of chemicals known as Phthalates have been linked to developmental and reproductive problems and risks. The cosmetics industry maintains that these chemicals are safe, but many companies have quit using them in response to public pressure and concern. Avon, Sally Hansen, Cover Girl, L'Oreal, Max Factor and Revlon have all reformulated some of their lines in response to concerns. The problem is, phthalates are not required to be listed on labels and so you'll never know if you are using them. They are very common in fragrances and products such as hair sprays, lotions, and deodorants.

In truth, scientists are just now beginning to understand the effect of phthalates on our bodies, as it increasingly becomes clear that these chemicals are lodging in our bodies from using these products. Recent studies have found breakdowns of these chemicals in every person studied.

Fortunately, many companies are reformulating products. This is at least partially in response to a European Union ban on more than 1,000 additives to cosmetics (in contrast, the United States has outlawed only 8 additives). It makes good financial sense for companies to comply with the EU ban so that they can sell their products overseas, too. Approximately 380 companies have signed a pledge vowing to get their products in line with the European Union guidelines. And, California recently passed a law requiring cosmetics companies with a million dollars or more in sales to report products containing carcinogenic or toxic chemicals.

These changes will have a beneficial effect for consumers, but bear in mind that phthalates are not illegal and some companies will continue to use them. You can read labels, which helps some, though not a lot, because not all chemicals are required to be listed. It's helpful to avoid products that list "fragrance" as that is often where phthalates are added. Bear in mind, though, that even products listed as "fragrance-free" may have phthalates in them because often some sort of fragrance is added to mask the smell of chemicals.

For more information and helpful resources such as brand comparisons, check out the website of the Environmental Working Group (www.ewg.org), this should help you make some wise choices.

Shop Green Action Steps

- Remember the three Rs when shopping
- Buy products with less packaging
- Shop at farmer's markets
- Take the Eat Local challenge
- Buy green cleaning supplies
- Choose green personal care products and cosmetics

Plant Green Things

 One of the most satisfying ways to become a steward of the planet is to plant a garden. You can grow flowers to beautify indoors and out or vegetables to help to sustain your family's food or both. Even if you aren't interested in maintaining a garden, you can also plant native plants to cut down on the amount of watering that is necessary and contribute to the health of the earth. But many people these days are turning to organic gardening and permaculture to tend their backyards or front yards, for that matter.

 Let's begin with organic gardening which at its simplest can be defined as gardening without chemicals. It's interesting to consider that it's only for the last few decades that anything other than organic gardening was performed on the planet. Farmers and gardeners worked the soil through organic means for millennia. But then in the 1920s, mass farming became more and more the means through which our food was grown, and it depended on high yields, quick growth and more profitable methods. This came to mean reliance on chemicals and fertilizers with little care or concern for the long-term impact of these products. And these ideas spilled over to urban and suburban gardeners, who wanted the greenest lawns, and the lushest roses with little concern for the consequences of the chemicals they used.

But many commercial pesticides such as DDT have been outlawed and gradually more and more attention has been paid to the pitfalls of mass farming and gardening with chemicals. Now most home gardeners would agree that organic gardening is the way to go, and it has come to mean a whole approach to gardening that is a balanced way of looking at things.

One of the cornerstones of organic gardening is using compost, and we've already discussed that at length in the section on recycling. Just be aware that if you've not used compost in your garden before, you are in for a big surprise at how much your plants will like it. You can easily say no to chemical fertilizers if you practice integrated pest management. And you can say goodbye to weeds using the techniques of weed-free garden design.

There are other cornerstones to organic gardening. They include learning to understand and mimic nature, which involves looking at your garden as a whole, functioning system; celebrating diversity, and growing each plant in a natural location for it. You can also apply organic gardening to lawn care with a few simple principles: use a natural, organic fertilizer; don't over water; aerate; mow high, and control bugs naturally.

There are many, many resources available for organic gardening. Start by going to www.organicgardening.com, the online site of the venerable magazine published by Rodale. This magazine was beating the drum for organic gardening back when everyone thought we good achieve better living through chemicals.

Another offshoot of the organic gardening boom is the heirloom seed movement. Small companies and organizations have grown up over the last couple of decades which are dedicated to preserving not only heirloom and rare seeds and plants, but also to maintaining biodiversity. One of the leaders in the field is Seeds of Change (www.seedsofchange.com) which has worked to promote biodiversity and promote sustainable, organic agriculture since 1989. They do this through cultivating open-pollinated, rare and heirloom seeds for flowers, herbs, and vegetables.

Due to the rapid consolidation of the seed industry and the decline of indigenous farming cultures, many traditional and heirloom seeds have been in danger of becoming extinct. An example of this is a statistic listed on the website: historically, we used over 7,000 species for food. But now, 20 species provide 90% of our diet. But groups and companies like Seeds of Change are actively working to change this through selling seeds and a research farm. They have also expanded their product line to include gardening tools, books and a while group of organic foods.

Another group is Seed Savers (www.seedsavers.org) which was begun in 1975. It is a non-profit organization dedicated to preserving the heritage of heirloom seeds and was begun when Diane Whealy and Kent Whealy were given the seeds to two garden tomatoes that had been brought to the United States from Bavaria in the 1870s. This made them realize how precious heirloom seeds are and how they need to be protected. Seed Savers also maintains a demonstration farm and it is dedicated to collecting, conserving and sharing heirloom seeds and plants and also to educating people about them.

A trend that is growing along with organic gardening is permaculture. What is permaculture? You'll find as many definitions as you do practitioners, but the term, which combines the words "permanent" and "agriculture" was coined in 1975 by Australian Bill Mollison. The basic idea  is that of working with nature to create a sustainable system: "permaculture is a philosophy of working with, rather than against nature; of protracted and thoughtful observation rather than protracted and thoughtless labor; of looking at plants and animals in all their functions, rather than treating any area as a single-product system."

Permaculture is about the design of an ecologically sound way of living, both indoors and out, at home and at work. Many of the principles of permaculture have been adopted around the world, especially in developing countries, where they are an extremely useful model. A book you might want to check out is called *Permaculture: Principles and Pathways Beyond Sustainability* by David Holmgren, co-originator of the permaculture concept. *Permaculture in a Nutshell*, by David Whitehall, is a very inexpensive ($9) introduction to the subject. A good place to buy books online is www.100fires.com, if you are interested in alternatives to the big online retailers.

While we are on the topic of planting green things, let's not forget trees. We have learned all throughout this report about the devastating consequences of global warming and how it is in many ways unstoppable unless we stop our actions and change our ways. One of the best ways to restore our air and ecosystem is to plant trees. Why? Because trees take  in carbon dioxide and change it to oxygen, then releasing more pure oxygen into the air. Trees function as the lungs of our planet. According to Coloradotree.org, about 800 million tons of carbon is stored in the trees of the urban forests of the U.S. That's a lot of carbon! A mature tree can absorb up to 48 pounds of carbon dioxide a year, and in turn releases enough oxygen for 2 people

And, beyond that, they create habitat for birds and other wild creatures and they are aesthetically pleasing as well. They help restore ozone levels in urban areas and reduce runoff and erosion. They absorb sound, reduce noise pollution, and create shade. And, trees have repeatedly been shown to improve both mental and emotional health and physical health of people. With all these benefits, you can understand why planting trees is such an eco-friendly activity.

Trees are great energy savers. Trees cool your home—the Arbor Day Foundation says that the shade of one tree can have the same effect as running 10-room size air conditioners for 20 hours. Trees can also act as windbreaks for your home and help to save on energy costs.

 You can easily join in the tree-planting. It's easy to plant a tree in your backyard. Do a little bit of online research and then visit a local nursery, where employees can help you choose a tree that will best suit your location and needs. There are so many beautiful trees, and they are adaptable for different uses.

You can also join in a more massive tree-planting drive, or donate money to one. The National Arbor Day Foundation (www.arborday.org) "inspires people to plant, nurture, and celebrate trees." In 2006, member planted over 8.5 million trees. When you join the Arbor Day foundation, you receive 10 trees and a book explaining about all aspects of planting and caring for them. You will receive either 10 flowering trees or 10 Oak trees. They can be delivered to your home, or some other address, such as your place of worship or business. Or, you can join the foundation and not receive the trees. You can also donate to the Arbor Day Foundation's project to reclaim forests devastated by fire. Extreme drought conditions have created problems in our national forests, and many acres of it have burned. For every dollar you donate to this cause, the foundation can plant one tree. Another very important project is donating money to help replant trees in New Orleans, which was devastated by Hurricane Katrina. Again, for every dollar you donate, one tree can be planted. Other projects include the rain forest rescue and trees for western New York, which was devastated by an early snowfall, which killed many trees.

The Arbor Day Foundation is probably best known for its namesake day—Arbor Day. Nationally, this day is the last Friday in April, but many states have their own dates for Arbor Day. Check the website for details and activities, which include many celebrations. This year, the foundation is partnering with Home Depot to plant 1,000 trees in 10 cities across the nation.

One of the extraordinary projects of the Arbor Day Foundation is the 50 Million tree initiative. This is a public-private partnership. Enterprise Rent-A-Car marked its 50th birthday in February 2007, and to celebrate, they pledged to plant 50 million trees in tandem with the Arbor Day Foundation, over the next 50 years. In a gift that totals over $50 million dollars, Enterprise plans to plant one million trees a year.

Another national group, American Forests (www.americanforests.org) works to protect, restore and enhance forests and trees. American Forests has teamed with Ikea to promote and plant trees. The average American family needs to plant 30 trees to offset their carbon emissions produced by their daily energy use. Ikea's focus is to plant enough trees to offset the number of cars driving to and from their stores. They plan to plant about 33,100 trees a year, enough to offset the carbon emissions from employees and visitors to their stores.

You can go to the Carbon Calculator page on the American Forests website and fill in estimates about your power usage, and then calculate how many trees you need to plant to offset your carbon emissions. Then all you have to do is donate money to equal the planting of that number of trees. It's an easy way to offset your carbon emissions and feel good about preventing global warming.

One of American Forest's biggest programs is Global Releaf. Begun in 1988, it is an education and action program that has planted over 23 million trees for environmental restoration since its inception.

Since trees are the earth's lungs, you can see how important it is to replant them. And easy, too—since both major tree-planting organizations plant a tree for each donation of one dollar, it doesn't take much to make a difference.

Plant Green Things Action Steps
- Plant an organic garden
- Grow an organic lawn
- Buy heirloom seeds
- Look into permaculture
- Plant trees!
- Calculate carbon emissions and buy trees to offset.

Become an Activist

It is very difficult, if not impossible, to read a report like this, become aware of the extent of the problem, and not become immediately inspired to take action. The purpose of this report has been to show you how doing just a few simple little things can make a huge difference, and that taking some steps beyond the little things can have an even bigger impact. But what if you want to go a step further? What if you are so concerned that you want to become a global warming activist?

The first thing to do is educate yourself. Read and study this report, and visit all the websites that are mentioned. Visit your local library for books, or go to Amazon or 100fires.com to find titles. Read magazines and stay up on the news about global warming. It's easy to find information these days because it's a hot topic (no pun intended). People are waking up to the fact that we are in a huge crisis and we need to do things to stop it right now.

Start a blog

There are many ways to spread the word after you have educated yourself. One simple and effective way is to start a blog. You can go to blogger.com and create a free blog for yourself, or go to typepad.com and get one for nominal price per month. It's easy to set up and post to a blog, and it is an effective way to get information out. Send the link to all our friends and colleagues with a note about why you felt the need to begin the blog. For content, you can write about your own efforts to become greener, at home and at work, what is going on in your community as well as the wider world. You can provide links to websites and resources where people can learn more, and you can create lists of books and magazines for more information.

Along these same lines, you can make a page at Squidoo (www.squidoo.com). What's a Squidoo? It's an interactive website, a huge conglomeration of web pages, really, on all subjects. It's user friendly and easy to create pages. You can link to other like-minded individuals through the group feature, and make some connections with other activists. And you can send traffic to your blog.

Join an organization

Going a step further, there are many, many organizations which you can join, and you will find and extensive list in the resource pages which follow this report. At the Stop Global Warming website, you can sign a petition to join a virtual march—which is now over 700,000 strong. From the website you can link to the Roots online store (http://usa.roots.com) where for $5 you can buy an attractive bracelet. 100% of the proceeds from the sale of the bracelet go to the Stop Global Warming Fund.

Global Green, the US arm of the Green Cross organization founded by Mikhail Gorbachev, is another excellent group which links its work on global warming to activism on water resources and eradicating weapons of mass destruction. Another excellent group is Environmental Defense (www.environmentaldefense.org). Their website is chock-full of resources and information. You can sign up to get Action Alerts about events that need your attention. If you fill in your address, the group will also keep you informed of local activities and events.

Each organization will have a slightly different focus, and slightly different activities, but all of them are actively working to fight the threat of global warming. Spend some time perusing the list at the end of this report and find an organization that suits your needs.

Kyoto Protocol

As mentioned earlier, the *Kyoto Protocol* is an international and binding agreement that many are entering into as a way to reduce greenhouse gases worldwide. While the current United States administration has not yet signed the accord, many cities in the U.S. have taken it upon themselves to do so. As of May 3, 2007, 496 US cities in 50 states, representing over 60 million Americans, have signed the accord, which was the brainchild of Seattle mayor Greg Nickels.

What this means for individual cities is that each of them will produce a greenhouse gas inventory and a plan on how to reduce it. This may include running municipal vehicles on electricity, planting trees, investment in renewable energy, improving public transportation and providing bike lanes. New York mayor Michael Bloomberg wants to reduce emissions from the city's vehicle fleet by purchasing hybrid cars.

If you, like most scientists and many elected officials, believe that the Kyoto Protocol is sound policy, contact your local city government to find out if they have signed the protocol. You can find a list of which mayors have signed at Stop Global Warming. You can also visit the official site of the US Mayor Climate Protection Agreement at www.seattle.gov/mayor/climate. And if they haven't signed, you might begin an education program to tell them why they should. You can also visit the website of the Kyoto USA group (www.kyotousa.org) which is a grass roots effort to encourage cities to take action to address the crisis of global warming.

Become an Activist Action Steps

- Get Informed
- Start a blog
- Make a Squidoo page
- Join organizations
- Support the Kyoto Protocol

What Will You Choose To Do?

Once you become interested in global warming and start to read and understand the extent of the problem, it is impossible to sit idly by any longer. It's unlikely that you will be able to return to some of your own previous habits. Simply reading a few pages of this report will likely have you turning off appliances and switching out light bulbs. You might even be inspired to buy a hybrid car or bike to work. Perhaps you will start an organic garden in your backyard or learn about permaculture. For sure you'll be more careful about what you allow to wash down storm drains, and you'll probably begin a more extensive recycling program in your home.

Any and all of those activities and others listed in this report will help. The only thing that won't help is if you sit back again and do nothing. There are way too many people in this country and others who don't know understand the parameters of the problem. Now that you do, it's up to you to take action. Whether you are 20 or 80 our future and the future of our children and grandchildren depend on it.

Resources

General

Start here for general websites that will have many resources, links, and information. These are all excellent references. Many of them have options to join to receive newsletters and other reports. The best way to keep in touch with what's going on is to sign up for these newsletters.

- Earth 911   www.earth911.org
- Environmental Defense www.environmentaldefense.org
- Stop Global Warming www.stopglobalwarming.org
- Global Green www.globalgreen.org
- Treehugger www.treehugger.com
- Green Options www.greenoptions.com

Government and Official Sites

Go to these sites for official news and information. They are detailed and full of useful information, if a bit densely written at times.

- US Department of Energy www.energy.gov/greenpower
- US Global Change Research Program www.usgcrp.gov
- United Nations Framework Convention on Climate Change http://unfcc.int
- World Health Organization www.who.int
- Fuel economy standards www.fueleconomy.gov

Green Commuting

These sites offer a wide variety of information on hybrid cars, fuel efficiency, mass transit, walking, and bicycling.

- www.hybridcars.com

- http://autos.yahoo.com

- www.greenercars.com

- www.fueleconomy.gov

- www.flexcar.com

- www.zipcar.com

- www.bikeleague.org

- www.biketowork.com

- www.bikecommute.com

- www.bikemonth.com

- www.walking.org

- www.walking.about.com

- www.shorewalkers.org

- Volkswalking US www.ava.org

- Volkswalking Canada www.walks.ca

Be Green at Work

- www.greenatworkmag.com

- www.greenatworktoday.com

- Offsets at work www.itm.org.uk

- LEED www.usgbc.org

Recycling

- www.christmastree.org

- www.earth911.org

- www.realchristmastrees.org

- www.compostguide.com

- www.composters.com

- www.mastercomposter.com

- www.epa.gov/compost

- www.recyclebindesigns.com

- www.retroactif.com

- www.escama.com

- www.greenmuseum.org

Shop Green

- www.farmersmarkets.com

- www.ams.usda.gov/farmersmarkets

- www.eatlocal.net

- www.ecolabel.org

- www.seventhgeneration.com

- www.mrsmeyers.com

- www.shaklee.com

- Environmental Working Group www.ewg.org

Plant Green Things

- www.organicgardening.com

- www.journeytoforever.org

- www.organicgardeningtips.com

- www.permaculture.org

- www.permanentpublications.co.uk

- www.permaculture.net

- www.seedsavers.org

- www.heirloomseeds.com

- www.seedsofchange.com

- www.arborday.org

- www.americanforests.org

- www.friendsoftrees.org

- www.sustainableharvest.org

- www.seattle.gov/mayor/climate
- www.blogger.com
- www.typepad.com
- www.squidoo.com
- www.climatesolutions.org
- Natural Resources Defense Council www.nrdc.org
- www.sierraclub.org
- www.kyotousa.org
- www.climatecrisicoalition.org